SECOND

TO

NONE

Book III of the
End of Tour Series

Pete Thron

SECOND TO NONE

Book III : End of Tour Series

Published in the United States of America

Copyright 2021 by Pete Thron

ISBN: 979-8-88589-354-1

THE END OF TOUR SERIES

ACKNOWLEDGEMENTS

I'd like to thank the company Blue Line Beasts for allowing me to use their logo for the cover of the book. Dedication

Dedication

This book is dedication to two people in my life that will always be my angels.

My beautiful little granddaughter Michelle Corr and my amazing, beautiful Aunt Marie Paganini. Heaven has gained two angels. Thank you for all the incredible times and memories you both provided to me and our family.

Table of Contents

Warning:

This book contains graphic descriptions of crimes and adult language. Some of the material in this book might trouble some readers.

The text includes sexual situations, rape, vivid violence, substance abuse, homelessness, profane or explicit language, and political views.

It is intended for mature readers.

Prologue

This book is dedicated to the men and women of law enforcement around the world. Imagine if you would, the weight of a person's conscience the pressure these amazing individuals feel every day. They kiss their wives, husbands, and children goodbye, before they leave for their shift, knowing that this may be the last time they'll ever see their loved ones again.

Law Enforcement officers wear many different hats while performing their duties. One tour they'll be arresting a violent criminal and might be fighting for their life in the process of putting that violent offender into custody. The next day they're a psychiatrist talking a person off the ledge of a high-rise building. Their day could be going smoothly and the very next second, they're driving up to a burning building. These brave individuals will rush into the building unprotected from the inferno and pull the occupants out from the blaze.

For a second, I'd like you to put the book down and close your eyes and imagine that you're in a police cruiser and your car has been dispatched to a violent felon who's armed with a firearm. You pull up to the scene and he's got a gun pressed against a little child's head. You've got your weapon out and you're shouting commands for him to drop his weapon and release the child. In a split second, he throws the child down to the ground and fires at you. You've got maybe a tenth of a second to react and return fire to protect yourself and the child. These are some of the split-second decisions these blue heroes are faced with every day they pin that shield on and put their weapons into their holsters.

I've written two books about some of my encounters and know firsthand what it's like to hold these burdens inside and keep all the horrors that a cop faces each and every moment of their lives. Law enforcement is such a highly stressful job and can eat at the officer's soul. God bless and Godspeed to them all and thank you for your service. These are their amazing stories.

There's a saying that I lived by during my career as a police officer. The job puts you into these places and incidents where the wrong thing becomes the right thing. And the right thing can become the wrong thing. The only ones that will have your Six is your brothers and Sister in Blue.

CHAPTER I

Retired NYPD Sergeant: Gregory Quinn

Greg Quinn has worn many shields in his lifetime, starting when he was in grammar school. Even at a youthful age, blue blood coursed through Greg's veins. Despite hating school, he still performed his duties with pride. Over the years, he received several awards from his principal for his diligence in completing his assignments. He became a school safety patrol crossing guard in

Ridgewood, a pleasant neighborhood that straddles the line between Queens and Brooklyn in New York.

Today, Ridgewood is one of the safest neighborhoods in New York; but it wasn't always that way. In 1977, when he was sixteen, two armed robbers confronted a friend and Greg attempted to save him. The robbers shot Greg in the chest. Due to the trauma he suffered from the gunshot wound, the doctors didn't expect him to survive. The priest read him his last rites. Greg refused to stop fighting and survived despite the severity of his wound.

While the injury prevented him from returning to public school, when he turned 18, he tested and received his GED. After that, it was a natural decision to become an auxiliary cop in 1979. He logged in over 2500 hours while performing his sworn obligation to protect the citizens of New York. During this time, he remained unarmed while performing his duties as an auxiliary police officer. This didn't prevent him from making more arrests than many of the uniformed members in the division where he was assigned. This was often major collars, such as rape, robbery, guns, and burglary. During his service as an auxiliary cop, they awarded him several medals, including the Medal of Valor, five merit awards and five additional commendations.

In 1983, he was appointed to the NYC Transit police and rolled over to the NYPD in 1984. He rose through the ranks over the next four years, becoming a sergeant in 1988. Unfortunately, a change in educational requirements forced a demotion in rank in 1991 because of his lack of college credits. Six years later, the rules were modified, and they reinstated his rank of Sergeant in 1997, before he vested out in 1998. During his time on the job, he was involved in five shootings, four with armed perpetrators and one with an attack dog. He received numerous medals for his bravery. 1 exception merit, 4 commendations, 22 meritorious awards, and 52 excellent police duty awards, along with 2-unit citations and a few, cop of the month citations in various commands.

These are his stories.

Incident one:

On December 4, 1978, at 2:10 pm, Greg Quinn was walking with a friend (henceforth identified as John) to the Social Security Administration in Jamaica, Queens. He needed to obtain a duplicate social security card. As the two young men walked along 161st Street, two males in their early 20s approached them. Both males were wearing snorkel coats with large hoods. Greg and John realized there was something about their behavior that made them uncomfortable. The assailants became aggressive, showing they were armed with handguns. One man carried a revolver in his hand. The second man opened his coat wide enough to allow them to view an automatic handgun. The assailants instructed Greg and his friend John to enter an enclosed staircase area that opened to a courtyard behind the building. Greg hesitated. He knew the danger would increase if they stepped out of public sight. He responded to their commands, stating, "There's no way we're fucking going down those steps." Both men knew in their guts that the enclosed courtyard was a deathtrap. Realizing that every second they remained on the street increased the chances of discovery, the perp with the automatic firearm tried to push his friend down the stairs.

Greg immediately grabbed for the perp's firearm.

After a brief struggle, he couldn't gain control of the gun itself, but Quinn was able to disable it by jacking the slide back. It was at that moment the second perp with the revolver started to pistol whip John on his head. John fell to the ground, dazed. Greg quickly wheeled around and wrestled with the second perp for possession of the gun. Because of the man's larger size and the puffiness of the armed felon's coat, he was having trouble getting his hands on the revolver. The fight flowed into the street and the perp was able to break free from Greg's grip. He fired a shot that hit him in his right shoulder before traveling in an upward direction to strike his collarbone. The bone fragmented the bullet and sent several fragments into his right lung. After he shot him, Greg quickly ducked behind a nearby car, which deflected additional rounds that were being fired at him. As the sound of approaching sirens grew louder, both perpetrators fled the scene empty handed. Greg leaned against the car waiting for assistance to arrive; worried as he began vomiting bile and coughing out blood.

A livery cab who had witnessed the shooting knew the teen needed medical help soon or he wouldn't make it. He hailed down a patrol car from the 103 precinct. The officers didn't wait for an ambulance. He immediately transported them to Mary Immaculate hospital. Despite all the blood, John had suffered a minor concussion. Greg's condition was dire. The metal shards had damaged several pulmonary blood vessels. He was basically drowning in his own blood, suffocating from the severe wounds to his lung.

Despite being rushed into surgery, the emergency room staff feared he wouldn't survive the operation. When his condition worsened, they had a priest come into the operating room and administer Greg's last rites during the surgery. Forever a fighter, Greg survived. Several weeks later, he'd recovered and was back home with his family. That bullet is still in his right lung to this day. These are his words, *"Strange what you think about at such moments. When I was in the back seat of the police cruiser, my mind thought about the movie Serpico when Al Pacino was being transported to the hospital after being shot in the face."*

***

I completely understand Greg's thinking. When I had been pistol whipped during an arrest, I originally thought they had shot me in my face and the same movie came to mind. I guess the movie Serpico had a major impact on our careers as cops. I truly can't imagine the raw courage of this young man who'd put his life on the line for his friend. It's truly an amazing story. Years later, his colleagues would dub him, The Mighty Quinn.

Incident Two:

As an auxiliary cop, Officer Quinn made an off-duty arrest for the violent crime of rape. It occurred while he was assigned to the 112 Precinct in Queens on February 14, 1982. Quinn had agreed to meet a few friends at a local movie theater on Queens Boulevard after his shift ended. Even during his off-duty hours, he had a habit of monitoring his police scanner as he was driving. That night, as he headed up Yellowstone Boulevard toward the movie theater, a call came over the radio. He listened, noting that the Anti-Crime Unit of the 112 Precinct called in a possible burglary in process. The report noted a suspicious male dressed in dark clothing had been sighted on a fire escape near 71st. It appeared he was trying to break into an apartment.

Quinn's instinct told him to park in an empty lot near the LIRR overpass off Yellowstone Boulevard. The open ground beside the railroad tracks would allow the suspect to travel through the area without needing to travel on public streets. He parked his vehicle in a lot beyond the tracks, and about a block from the 112 Precinct in case they needed backup. Sure enough, a few minutes later, the radio reported the crime unit was in a foot pursuit of the prowler. The unknown suspect was traveling along the railroad tracks and heading in his direction. Within minutes, the perp appeared. Without warning, he ran away from the tracks and down toward a wooded area near the overpass. Quinn knew if the man reached the overgrown area, it would be difficult to locate him in the dark. He could see that the perp was carrying a knife in his hand. Thinking fast, he moved to intercept the suspect before he reached the wooded area. When he confronted him, he held his right hand on his hip, suggesting the presence of a holster and handgun. The perp hesitated, looking back toward the officers, who were fast approaching the area on foot.

Officer Quinn ordered the perp to drop the knife and lay down flat on the ground. The perp weighed his options and cursed, but he dropped the knife, then lay down. Officer Quinn kicked the knife away from him, then he handcuffed his wrists and took the perp into custody. He helped the man to his feet and walked him back toward his personal vehicle. Minutes later, Officer Quinn was able to hail down a patrol car to help him. The patrol officer laughed when he heard Quinn had bluffed the suspect into dropping his weapon and surrendering. He alerted the station that Quinn had the perp in custody and requested transport.

The supervisor on the scene ran a name check on the suspect. It turned out that the perp had outstanding warrants for multiple suspected assaults (rapes at knifepoint). Quinn offered to walk back and collect the knife while the supervisor completed the initial paperwork. Quinn's actions enabled the detectives to close several open rape cases. The suspect was charged and later convicted of multiple assault charges, including aggravated rape with a knife.

If Quinn hadn't used his intuition to park near the train tracks, the fleeing violent offender would've escaped that night and continued to rape women in the neighborhood. Greg Quinn would later receive a letter of commendation and the Medal of Valor for his actions.

Incident Three:

Quinn was still working as an auxiliary cop in the 102 precinct. He'd just finished the last day of a 4 X 12 tour and was driving home, thinking about the steak he'd left marinating in the refrigerator. As was his usual habit, he'd been listening to his police scanner. A call came over radio, announcing the report of a female screaming for help. The caller said he'd heard the screams near Park Lane South and 100th Street. This was in the Forest Park neighborhood of Queens. Now 100th Street ends at the Atlantic Substation, but at this time they hadn't planted the wooded strip that now runs from Atlantic to the park.

Being close to the location, Quinn went into action.

He'd been running behind at the end of shift and by chance was still wearing his uniform. He arrived on the scene in less than a minute. There he spoke with the complainant who'd called in the alert. Dispatch advised Officer Quinn that the witness had heard screams in the wooden area of the park. The Precinct patrol car arrived on the scene, and they began a grid search of the area. Several minutes later, Quinn heard scuffling and screams. He had his flashlight out and was searching through the heavy underbrush in the area. Suddenly, a man came running out of the woods from the area near where the complainant had heard the woman scream. Quinn tackled him. After a brief struggle, he was able to contain and handcuff the suspect. A second suspect was taken into custody in the woods by the officer in the patrol car. The patrol officer located the young woman, released her from the cuffs and then requested transported by ambulance to the hospital.

At the emergency room, the seventeen-year-old victim related the following to the patrolmen. "I was walking home alone from a friend's house. As I passed the outside edge of the park, two men grabbed me. They were not much older than me. I screamed for help as they dragged me into the woods about 100 feet away from the sidewalk. Once they had me in the woods, they threatened to kill me if I didn't stop screaming. I could tell they meant what they said, so I stayed as quiet as possible. They had handcuffs and cuffed my wrist to a small tree, so I couldn't get away. One man help my loose arm down as the other man raped me. At first, I was crying, and fighting with them. Then I just kept my eyes closed and lay still until it was over. Once they finished, they started discussing what to do with me. One was ready to leave, but the other insisted they needed to kill me to keep me from identifying them. They were about to strangle me with my own belt when the officer's light scared them."

During his search, Officer Quinn had startled them. The perpetrators saw his uniform when the rays of his flashlight caught his leg. They stopped trying to strangle the victim and placed their hands over her mouth to muffle any screams. She heard them say, "Stay quiet, bitch, and don't make a sound." The two men were afraid to move and hoped the uniform cop would leave the area without noticing them. But the sector car was also searching the area nearby. Fear of discovery forced the two felons to leave her and attempt to flee the crime scene. They split up since she would tell the police to look for two young men together.

"If I hadn't arrived on the scene when I did, she'd be another rape and murder statistic."

Incident Four:

In 1984, Greg Quinn was a Transit cop working in the subways. As part of the NYC Transit police, the Rockaway Round Robin A-line was his beat. The Beach 44th Street station, also known as Beach 44th Street–Frank Avenue station, is the last stop of the A-train on the Rockaway Line. Then it goes through the round-robin and returns to the central station.

At 0200 hours, what had been a quiet night ended just after the train pulled out of the Frank Ave/ Beach Street station. Office Quinn was riding in one of the subway cars and heard a shot. The train jolted to a sudden stop. A passenger came running into the subway car yelling, "They shot the conductor," and "the men that shot him jumped off the train in between the subway cars."

Quinn immediately radioed for medical help for the conductor, any available backup, and ran after the perps. Logic told him the men were familiar with the area, so he ran toward the station staircase leading to the street. As he exited the stairway, he spotted two men running across a field toward Beach 46th Street. He knew he'd have to make up the distance between him and the fleeing suspects. His radio relied on the transit systems shortwave system, so the transmitter wasn't working while he was on the city streets. He was on his own and in a full-fledged foot pursuit of two armed felons. As he turned the corner onto Beach 46 Street, he realized the area had multiple locations someone could easily ambush him. Seconds later, Quinn was met with a volley of five shots from a .45-caliber handgun. Only the fact that he was running kept him from being hit. He fired one shot at the perps and took cover behind a parked car.

The two men ran behind a series of buildings, dark alleys, and yards with Quinn pursuing them. Several minutes later, several cruisers from the 101st Precinct arrived on the scene. The desk officer and Duty Captain from Quinn's District also arrived on the scene. He related what had occurred to them. They seemed doubtful of officer Quinn's version, as the conductor had no visible injury. They interviewed the conductor who had said nothing unusual had occurred on the train. However, he had no explanation for the sudden abrupt stop.

The supervisors then inspected the subway cars and found a fresh bullet indentation near the conductor's window. They re-interviewed the conductor, who recounted his first statement and told them that two males were spitting on the train, and he had told them to stop. After the men exited the train, they fired a shot at the subway car as it left the station. He told them that the transit officer immediately got off the train and pursued the armed men.

They asked the conductor. "Why did you lie during the first interview?"

His response was, "It wasn't unusual. It happens to me all the time."

The investigators recovered the shell casing on the platform and three more in the street. There were several small droplets of blood found in the area where they were last seen as Officer Quinn had fired at them. Unfortunately, no one showed up at any of the hospitals with gunshot wounds. Despite multiple extensive investigations, the suspects were never located.

Incident Five:

In the summer of 86, Quinn was working in the 30 precinct, which is located in the western portion of New York just outside Harlem. Washington Heights and Sugar Hill are the primary neighborhoods covered by the 30. A large section of Riverside Park and Jackie Robinson Park are inside the 30 territory.

Officer Quinn had just returned from a well-needed vacation. The 30 had been busy while he was gone. There had been a string of robberies in the Midtown and Manhattan North areas. The suspect was robbing yellow cab drivers during the night hours of the 4x12 shifts. The perpetrator had committed over 40 robberies at gunpoint in the last two weeks, most happening while he was enjoying the beach. His M.O. (modus operandi) was to hail a cab in the Midtown area around Times Square and direct the driver to take him uptown, usually to an address in Harlem or Washington Heights. When the cabdriver pulled over to drop him off, he'd produce a handgun and rob him. He always made sure he was on a side street to avoid being seen. After he robbed one taxi, he'd locate another cab to drive him back down to Midtown. Then he would commit another gunpoint robbery of that driver. After he demanded them to hand over all their money, he would tell each driver. "If you love your wife and kids, you won't do anything stupid."

As is usually the results of a crime spree, the media got wind of it. It forced NYPD to launch a full-scale manhunt for the suspect in an area they preferred to ignore as much as possible. To satisfy the elected officials of the city, the Street crime unit, the Anti-crime unit, several robbery squads and multiple command level detectives were instructed to 'take any steps necessary' to nab the perpetrator.

After rollcall, Quinn told his partner Billy O'Brien (R.I.P.), "I've got a gut feeling this guy is going to strike again tonight in the Riverside Drive area of our command." As soon as they got into their patrol car, Quinn and his partner headed to Riverside Drive and the lower geographical part of their command. A short time later, as they approached 135th Street, Quinn spotted a yellow taxi turning North onto Riverside Drive with a lone male passenger in the back. This was enough to draw his attention. It was rare to spot a yellow cab past 96th Street. O'Brien agreed with Quinn. He did a quick U-turn and followed the taxi. Quinn had kept his eye on the cab as they reversed direction. Almost as soon as the patrol car passed them by, the taxi turned down onto 137th Street. Quinn had a feeling it was the man wanted in connection to the robberies. Quinn told Billy, "Don't follow him down 135th. Let me out here and after you pass by, I'll walk down the street and try to spot him. I bet he's sitting somewhere out of sight, waiting for us to pass by. Go around the block and come in from the other end." As soon as Quinn walked up to the corner, he observed the taxi had pulled over to the right side of the street next to the curb. He waited until his partner passed by, then began working his way toward the parked cab. With his service revolver in his hand, he approached the rear passenger side of the vehicle. The taxi driver had the windows rolled down, and Quinn could hear what they were saying.

He was almost in position when the passenger pointed a black handgun at the driver's head, and said, "If you love you wife and children, you won't do anything dumb or stupid." Quinn recognized the perps' words. Just as they suspected, it was the serial robber. O'Brien car was now visible as it slowly made its way down the street toward the parked taxi. There was no way the perp could miss it. He never saw detective Quinn approaching the car. Quinn placed his service revolver against the perp's head and cocked the hammer back and told him, "If you love your wife and kids, you won't do anything stupid."

After the incident took place, Quinn realized how comical his statement was. Several things could have gone wrong. The perp surprised him when he simply dropped his gun on the car floor and said, "Congratulations, you just caught the Serial Taxi Robber." Then he started laughing. Quinn cuffed him, pleased that he gave up without forcing an altercation. The whole time the perp was laughing about how he'd stolen his tag line, and now he couldn't say it to any other victims.

Now Quinn and O'Brien had another problem to deal with. Under department rules, a patrolman is supposed to advise central of the arrest and wait for his patrol supervisor. They knew the anti-crime team would try to steal credit for their arrest. They were famous for doing that to the uniform police officers. There was no way that they were letting anyone take credit away from them. So, they didn't put it out over the air and just drove the perp back to the command. O'Brien and Quinn informed central they had One Under. The desk officer logged Quinn and O'Brien in as the arresting officers, but O'Brien made it clear Quinn had done the actual arrest. After the perp was booked and placed in holding, they informed the clerk who he was. It was only then that they transmitted over the air that the Taxi Serial Robber had been arrested during another gunpoint robbery by officers of the 30. Almost immediately, the anti-crime boss and his team were yelling over the radio to have them standby at their location. Which, of course, was the command.

Quinn said. "I could almost hear the steam coming from his ears when he transmitted back that they had already processed the collar."

For his valiant effort, Officer Quinn received a Meritorious Medal. That's the second lowest medal a NYPD cop can get. What a slap in his face. The guy collars a serial robber and that's the department's gratitude. Just a damn shame, as far as I'm concerned. If a detective or a special detail had taken the defendant down, they'd surely would've received a higher commendation. But it was just a patrolman doing his lawful duty.

Incident Six:

By January 19, 1991, Seargent Quinn had rolled over the NYPD. He had been living in his Middle Village home where he'd grown up. He loved Queens and was happy he'd been able to buy the house back from the earlier owners. At approximately 9:30 pm, he was driving home from a restaurant on his regular day off. As he passed a gas station around the corner from his home, he noticed two suspicious males on the corner of Metropolitan Avenue and Admiral Avenue. They appeared to be scoping out the gas station. Quinn noticed that as they walked past the place of business, they kept a keen eye on the gas attendant, who was pumping a customer's gas. Full-service stations were still common. Willing to give the two men the benefit of the doubt, Sergeant Quinn watched them for a while. His instinct told him they were casing the joint prior to committing a robbery, so he parked his car on 65th Street and hid behind some bushes, which gave him a clear view of the gas station.

Quinn couldn't believe his luck, when several minutes later, the two suspects left the corner and met up with a third male just a few feet from where he was hiding. He could easily hear the conversation between the three men. Their words indicated they were going to rob the gas station. They even pointed to where they intended to wait prior to the robbery. After they went over the plans to commit the robbery, they got into a dark vehicle and pulled away too quickly for Quinn to get the plate number. The strange thing was that they drove in the opposite direction from the gas station. Perhaps they intended to rob the station at a future time? Quinn went back to his car and drove over to the gas station. He identified himself as the police and asked the attendant what time they closed. Then he alerted the attendant of the possible robbery.

Back in those days, there weren't many folks who owned a cell phone. Quinn didn't want to be trapped in the office while waiting for the three men to commit the crime. Quinn explained to him that a robbery was imminent, and he would have no time to call for any type of aid when it occurred.

Quinn instructed the employee to act as if everything was normal. He would park his vehicle in the dry cleaners' lot across the street. "This is very important. If a robbery occurs, comply with all their demands and hand over the money. Then lock the office door and contact 911. To ensure your safety, I'll wait to confront the suspects after they've left the station grounds."

The off-duty cop had to turn off his car ignition, so that the exhaust fumes wouldn't be seen in the frigid cold. He knew it might be a long wait in the cold car, but he knew if he left, no one would be around to stop the robbery. After 11:30 pm, the station closed, and they hadn't appeared. He figured the perps had found a different target to rob that night. Just as he prepared to leave, a gas truck pulled into the station to make an unexpected fuel delivery. About a half hour later, the truck was through and pulled out of the station.

Officer Quinn turned his car back on and drove across the street to the gas station to speak with the attendant and to fuel up. The employee said the fuel delivery was normal, and he'd forgot to mention it. Now that he had completed the delivery, he was going to lock up for the night. He said to the attendant. "I'll wait for you to lock up just in case. I'm going to ride up the street, like I'm leaving, circle the block and be right back."

As Quinn was returning after circling the block, he noticed the three men that had been hiding under a car parked in a closed business near the gas station. He watched as they approached the station to rob the attendant. In less than a minute, they had the money and were ready to return to the car. When they spotted Quinn sitting there, they fled on foot, running down Admiral Avenue for about a block before turning into an extremely dark alleyway. The sky was cloudy and without the moon; it was almost pitch black. Quinn kept his headlights off to his jeep as he pursued the armed men down Admiral Avenue into the tenebrific alleyway. As he crept slowing down the gloomy alley, they met him with a barrage of bullets from a handgun and a 22-caliber rifle. The bullets riddled his windshield. These are Sergeant Quinn's words. "As I got out of my Jeep, it became a running gun battle. My five-shot revolver against their handgun and a rifle which held a thirty-round magazine. It was so dark that I had to use the flashes from earlier shots to line up my sights for the next round I fired. The perps became more illuminated as they reached the exit from the alley. I had one shot left and fired. It was then I observed one of them limping as he was running."

"The injured perp almost fell to the ground, but his accomplice helped him stay on his feet. I rushed to reload and engage again quickly, but by the time I reloaded my off-duty revolver and exited the alleyway, the perps were driving away in their getaway vehicle."

Quinn returned to check on the station clerk and found out he had put most of the money inside a floor safe, so they didn't get as much as they expected. Two 104th precinct detectives later picked the three men up at Laguardia Hospital. "One of them had a round from my .38 in his ankle. I could've sworn I'd hit him in the head, but I guess I missed. It wasn't for the lack of trying."

It turned out that this violent team of robbers had done many commercial and pedestrian robberies at gunpoint in the area over the past several months. One of which was a robbery of an off duty IAB Captain in his own driveway.

When it came to doing the job he loved, Sergeant Quinn was a true *Five Percenter*. The five percenters are the cops that love one thing, making as many arrests as possible. They are the cops that run towards the suspects, who are violent, and armed to the teeth. I'm glad to say I was one of them, and wish I'd had the opportunity to patrol the streets with this true-blue hero.

CHAPTER II

Retired NYPD Police Officer: Joe Marino

Joe has a long family history within the NYPD. I'll go into that later in the chapter. Officer Marino is one of the curators of the Patrol Borough in Queens South, (PBQS) where there are many NYPD historical displays dating back to the1800s. The museum takes up three floors of the building. Mannequins in vintage uniform stand guard over the historical galley. The exhibit has many articles and artifacts like antique police lights, sirens, uniforms, shields, and firearms. Joe and his team made sure that every inch of the three floors had some type of relic on them. It all started approximately ten years ago when Joe and his Sergeant asked for permission to display some memorabilia to enrich the interior of PBQS. Joe is one of the few police officers to have five consecutive generations serve within the NYPD. This gave him the idea to do the museum.

After they submitted the request, they'd received permission to move forward from the former Borough Commanding Chief, Thomas Dale. Chief Dale also added the most honorable task of designing and creating a 'Line of Duty Memorial' for those who'd made the ultimate sacrifice in PBQS.

To this day, Joe continues researching and preserving the rich history of the NYPD. You can find almost anything historically significant in the halls of the museum. No matter how obscure, it's probably inside that building. There are old call boxes that the officers would have used to call and check in with their respective Precinct. Old lanterns, police beds, batons from Highway, Mounted, Transit, and the Housing police divisions. There's also a section for the policewomen's original police matron's uniform and shield. A vintage switchboard highlights the communications display. To add to the collections' relevance, many of the items come from current and retired members of the service.

The second floor focuses on the rich history of the officers who wore the gold shield, those inquisitive investigators better known as the detectives. Many of the displays have information about famous crimes. Poster boards exhibit crime scene photos, news articles, and crime scene photos of famous detective cases.

Officer Marino's five generation family tree.

Police officer James O'Neill served from 1854 to 1876 with the 3rd Precinct at 81 Warren Street. He was officer Marino's 4th great grandfather.

Detective Charles F. Kane, served from 1912 to 1940. His final posting was at Modd 18th Division. He was officer Marino's second uncle.

Detective Francis A. O'Neill, 1922 to 1943. His final posting was the Modd 18th Division. He was officer Marino's great grandfather.

Patrolman William Huzar served from 1946 to 1967. He worked out of the 10th Precinct. He was officer Marino's grandfather.

Detective George Wasylchiow Served from 1950 to 1979. Worked in the Intelligence Division. He was officer Marino's great uncle.

Patrolman Peter Senenko served from 1951 to 1960. He worked out of the 14th Precinct. He was officer Marino's great uncle.

Detective James O'Neill Served from1955 to 1971. He worked out of the 17th Precinct Squad. He was officer Marino's great uncle.

Police Officer Joseph Marino Sr. Served from 1988 to 2013 with PBQS Operations. He was officer Marino's father.

Retired Police Officer. James Marino 2008 to 2019. He worked out of the 107th Precinct Squad.

That's an amazing family tree of NYPD detectives and cops. I'm quite sure Joe had no problems learning how to become a solid cop in the street with that family history.

Incident one:

Growing up is hard regardless of your environment. As the number of single-parent households grew, the need to work with and support under- supervised youths increased. It was the youth officer who worked with at-risk youth on a daily basis, acting as bridges between the community and the department.

In 1989, Joe Marino was the youth officer in the 107 Precinct. He and his partner, officer Gentson, were making their routine checks of the schools in the area when they saw a 19-year-old male who'd just been assaulted and robbed. The complainant was bleeding heavily from a slash wound he'd received from one of five attackers. The incident occurred around 3 p.m. on Highland Avenue in the Jamacia neighborhood of Queens. An ambulance transported the victim to Mary Immaculate hospital where he'd received 24 stitches in his head. After ensuring the victim was receiving medical care, the officers took statements from three additional witnesses. Then they began canvassing the area in their patrol car.

School had let out for the day and small groups of teenagers were a common occurrence. However, the witnesses had provided excellent physical descriptions of the five attackers, as well as their clothing. They could also give a direction in which the teens were traveling.

Just past 165th was the entrance to a popular neighborhood park. At this time of day, it was common to see teenagers gathered near the pond. While they were driving through the park, they observed five teenagers who fit the description that the victim and witnesses had given them. Officer Marino immediately called for backup. Seconds later, the wary teens bolted in different directions to evade being caught. Gentson pursued two of the attackers and Marino gave chase to the other three suspects. A 15-minute foot pursuit took place inside the Jamaica Highland Park. (Now Captain Tilly Park) It finally ended with Gentson apprehending the two perps he'd chased. When returning to the vehicle, he discovered

Marino had apprehended the trio he was pursuing. The witnesses positively identified the five suspects as the robbers.

Their command named both officers *cop of the month* for taking swift action and doing a solid on-the-scene investigation.

Incident two:

One family story Officer Marino was especially proud of, involving his great grandfather, happened in the 1920s. He didn't have the exact date but was certain of the facts.

Before Francis O'Neill joined the police force, he was a middleweight pugilist with an enviable reputation. Even the local gangsters respected him and gave him a wide berth. The incident occurred while Patrolman O'Neill was walking his regular foot post. During the early morning hours of his late-night shift, he heard the screams of a person yelling. "Fire, Fire! Please save Theresa." He looked around and spotted an ominous glow coming from the rooftop of a building on the corner of 110th Street and Second Avenue. Just as he pulled the lever of a firebox, a terrace door was flung open. Light cut through the darkness as a woman came dashing out wearing nothing except a night grown. She rushed up to O'Neill and begged him to save Theresa. She was in an upstairs room and wouldn't answer her calls.

Officer O'Neill didn't hesitate. He dashed up the blazing staircase and finally reached the bedroom door. Dense smoke filled the narrow hall outside the room. He checked the door, then kicked it open. Inside the room, he found Theresa lying on the floor, overcome by smoke inhalation. As he carried her to safety, he too was overcome—but not by the smoke. Officer O'Neill knew nothing about the young lady except her name. Even in the dim light, it was clear she was beautiful as a spring dawn on the Mediterranean Sea.

After the unusual introduction, O'Neill would often drop by to see her at her new home on Second Avenue. After the fire incident damaged the house, it forced the family to move. It's said that Francis lost his heart while saving the young woman named Theresa. He was determined to win hers. His comrades at the East 104th Street station house joked with him for his attentiveness, but he preserved. Finally, she admitted her mutual interest. The social arbiters of the East Side had stamped their approval for their courtship. Every police officer on the force was pulling for the heroic Irish patrolman, Francis O'Neill. She said yes, and he married Theresa Calderano later that year.

***

Francis O'Neill would later transfer to the plainclothes squad that battled prohibition. In the early part of January 1920, congress prohibited the production, transportation, and distribution of alcohol drinking, thereby enforcing the 18th Amendment, a Constitutional law that lasted until 1933. Police raids on suspect secret or bootleg breweries became common. Organized crime became experts at smuggling alcohol into the country. This brought about the rise of rumrunners as the men who delivered the illegal hootch were called. The Mafia had no qualms about operating illegal saloons and private clubs, called speakeasies across the city.

One night, while investigating a reported speakeasy, Officer O'Neill observed a touring car that was heading on Tenth Avenue just South of Thirty-First Street. There were four men riding in the car. As the vehicle passed him, O'Neill saw suspicious bundles in the back of the automobile. Two of the men wore caps pulled down over their eyes, making it difficult to identify them. All four men had dressed in dark clothing. O'Neill held his shield up to identify himself as a cop and ordered the car to stop. Instead, the vehicle sped up. Two of the men drew revolvers and began firing at him. O'Neill fired back at the occupants, but a bullet hit him in his wrist and was bleeding heavily. He fell onto the roadway as the vehicle sped away. Because of the amount of blood he'd lost, Officer O'Neill lost consciousness.

Witnesses to the shooting said there were at least a dozen shots fired. A few people carried the injured police officer into a nearby drugstore. A clerk applied a tourniquet around his wrist to stop the bleeding. Someone had reported the incident and a few minutes later, detectives arrived on the scene. They placed O'Neill into their car, and one drove him to the nearest hospital. Other detectives canvassed the area to see if any of the witnesses had written down the automobile's plate number. The detectives had no luck locating the touring car.

Later, O'Neill told the investigators that in the back of the automobile were many boxes that more than likely had illegal liquor in them. After recovering from his wound, Officer O'Neill was promoted to detective. He was one of several elite detectives that worked the Lindbergh baby kidnapping case. In summer 1934, he was credited with the takedown of Tri-State gang member Herbert 'Trigger' Meyers and disrupting a planned series of kidnappings. Meyers was guilty of the murder of Madeline Weldon in Richmond, Virginia. Meyers had taken part in many of the infamous cigarette and mail truck hijackings, along with William Davis, alias Walter Legensa; Arthur (Dutch) Misunas; William B. Phillips; Morris (Big George) Kauffman; and Robert Mais.

It's said that O'Neill sent six men to the electric chair during his time on the force. The newspaper reports called him Buck. He retired after serving twenty-three years with the NYPD. He earned seven citations, the Isaac Bell Medal for Valor and the Martin J. Sheridan Medal for Valor. One interesting note, he retired with a $1600.00 dollar a year pension, which is about what the average retiring officer would receive per month now as a pension.

That's one hell of a family of police officers. I would've loved to be at a family dinner with them, to hear some of their war stories.

CHAPTER III

Retired NYPD Detective: Michael Reiter

Incident One:

Detective Michael Reiter prided himself on being an extremely proactive police officer. One evening, while on robbery recon in a robbery prone section of Brooklyn, New York, he had an interesting on-the-job experience. While working near Park Place and Franklin Avenue, Detective Reiter noticed man exiting 522 Park Place, an upscale residential building. The suspect appeared to be nervous, constantly looking around, which drew the detective's attention. Upon further examination, Detective Reiter judged him to be carrying a handgun which was sticking out of his waistband.

Michael and his team exited their undercover vehicle and identified themselves as the police. The perp then pulled his weapon from his waistband and fled west on Park Place, dodging in and out of pedestrians on the sidewalk. He then turned south on Classon Avenue, passing Saint Theresa of Avila Church. Figuring the fugitive was heading for Prospect Park, two of the team members returned to the vehicle, planning on cutting him off at the Eastern Parkway.

Detective Reiter continued to pursue the suspect in an intense foot pursuit after he changed direction and cut through the grounds of PS 316. He was getting tired, and he figured the man he was chasing couldn't be doing much better. He expected the perp to look for a likely location to hide, hoping Reiter would miss him in the dark. He might have gotten away, except he stepped on a cat's tail in the dark, alerting Detective Reiter to his hiding spot. He finally apprehended the suspect with no shots being fired.

Once the perpetrator was cuffed, the detective discovered he was carrying a .38-caliber revolver, along with six vials of crack cocaine. While being escorted to the waiting transport, the defendant offered Detective Reiter a bribe for $600.00 and an additional $700.00 hidden elsewhere. He also included the .38-caliber handgun, and the crack cocaine in his bid for his release. Reiter ignored his offer and booked him in on December 16, 1987, at approximately 20:45 hours. However, the quick-thinking detective notified his boss and the Internal Affairs Division, who later that evening taped the defendant offering several officers in the R.I.P. unit money. The suspect would be convicted of bribery, possession of a firearm, possession of narcotics, and resisting arrest.

Incident Two:

October 20, 1987, at approximately 2045 hours, Detective Reiter was on robbery recon near Bedford Avenue and Bergen Street. He had received a tip of men planning a robbery from a Confidential Informant and wanted to check out the neighborhood. While cruising around the area, he observed a white male wanted for a robbery in the 77th precinct walking up Bedford Avenue toward Bergen Street. He immediately called the sighting in, then moved his vehicle forward. He knew the suspect was most likely armed and wearing a bulletproof vest. One thing ran through his mind, "Chances are extremely good that I'm going to be in a gunfight."

The perpetrator must have glimpsed his vehicle turning onto Bergen because he gave up any attempt to remain nonchalant and fled into the closest building, which was a four-story brick multi-unit at 992 Bergen Street. Reiter slid to a stop, and gave pursuit, charging into the building. He knew if the suspect could enter a unit, it would be much harder to capture him. The suspect was attempting to unlock the door of a basement level unit. Realizing he couldn't pull a gun while holding the keys, Reiter jumped over the railing, dropping down atop the suspect. A short but fierce struggle ensued, he was able to apprehend the perp, cuff him, and then disarm him. Later, at the station house, two victims positively identified the suspect as the perpetrator of past robberies against them.

A quick check found the defendant, John Simmons, was wanted in connection to several unsolved cases, including a homicide in the Brooklyn North precinct. He increased the scope of his interview and was able to link Simmons to several additional cases.

Once he had the additional files in hand, Detective Reiter released just enough info to scare the defendant and he rolled over, giving credible information on several other cases. Many of the cases involved several additional co-defendants.

This was just great police work on Mike's part. If he'd not been so persistent during the interview, those other cases may have never been closed out.

Incident Three:

One cold afternoon in January 1989, detective Reiter was on robbery surveillance near Rochester Avenue and Bergen Street after receiving a request from the New York Housing Authority for help with a rash of recent break-ins. The team was riding past the playground when he spotted a suspicious male moving awkwardly while crossing the street. He walked slowly and kept adjusting his waistband.

Reiter and his team exited their car and walked toward the suspect. As they got closer, Reiter saw the suspect had his hand on the handle of an automatic firearm. The perp pulled the gun out of his waistband and took a combat stance as he fired his weapon. The firearm jammed, giving Reiter and the others time to take cover and get ready to return fire. The problem was that they would be firing toward an elementary school that was just letting the children out for the day. As the perp continued firing shots at the three detectives, the men used all their restraint not to fire at the perpetrator. No one wanted a pedestrian caught in the crossfire.

The suspect realized the officers were not shooting back and fled, running back toward the school. Since his pants were sagging, he put the gun back in his waistband so he could hold his pants up as he ran. Reiter and one team member chased after the fleeing perp, while the third member of the team circled around the block in his vehicle. A foot pursuit took place up Bergen and ultimately the suspect was apprehended when surrounded by the three officers a few blocks down from the school. He'd tossed the gun into the grass while passing by the school playground, but Reiter's partner saw him toss it and picked it up.

The exhausted suspect was transported a short distance to the 77 precinct where he was processed in. While running the gun through operations, ballistics revealed the same gun had been used the gun in an armed robbery of a Lindenwood jewelry store. They placed the suspect into a line-up, and the owner of the jewelry store identified him. The defendant was charged with attempted murder of four police officers and a separate charge of armed robbery.

Once again, Reiter's instinct and experience took another felon off the street.

Incident Four:

In January 1990, Detective Reiter and his partner, Police Officer Barba, were assigned to the 77th precinct R.I.P. unit. (Robbery in progress) By this time, Reiter had become familiar with most of the neighborhoods in Brooklyn. When something out of the ordinary occurred, he was able to recognize it and make faster decisions on how to follow up. They were canvassing an area in East New York Brooklyn which was frequented by a known robbery suspect. At approximately 8:30 pm, the two plainclothes officers entered a multi-unit residential building in that area to question the residents about the suspect. As they entered one of the drug infested buildings, they saw a male standing in shadows beneath the staircase about halfway along the hallway. The man stepped back as they came through the door, as if he was trying not to be seen. They immediately announced themselves as police officers and said they would like to talk to him. They were about to show him a photo of the suspect when the man quickly turned and bolted toward the rear exit door.

Detective Reiter acted quickly and gave pursuit. He shouted the ordered for the unknown man to stop, but the suspect ignored his commands. Just before the door exiting the rear of the building, the suspect turned towards Michael with a pistol in his hand and fired directly at Detective Reiter. The bullet hit him square in his chest but was deflected by the shock plate which was inside his bulletproof vest. Despite being in immense pain Detective Reiter and his partner returned fire, fatally wounding the shooter. Had Detective Reiter not been wearing his bulletproof vest that tour, he'd surely been killed in the line of duty.

In his own words, Michael said, "I felt incredibly lucky that I was wearing my vest. I thank God I'm alive."

Incident Five:

In the fall of 1990, Detective Reiter and his partners in the R.I.P. unit were investigating an unsolved armored car robbery. The suspects had gotten away with close to $42,000.00 dollars and one of the guard's firearms. With very few clues as to the identity of the perpetrators, they were thinking the case might remain unsolved. There had been previous robberies enacted in a similar manner and even though there had been suspects named in the previous robberies, none had been declared in the September 23rd case.

Detective Reiter's team was conducting routine robbery surveillance within the confines of the 77th precinct on that tour. They were driving down Lincoln Place when Detective Reiter observed a male that was wanted in connection with the armored car robbery which had taken place on August 9th. Lincoln place was one of those streets that changed completely depending on which end you were on. The stately brownstones near Prospect Park were nothing like the multi-unit homes in the Weeksville area at the opposite end. The male suspect was spotted in front of 1226 Lincoln Place. He was carrying a bag and a pizza box and was walking casually. Reiter and Officer Barba exited the vehicle while his partner continued up the narrow one way, stopping about a hundred feet beyond the suspect.

Detective Reiter and Barba identified themselves as police. The suspect cooperated, and they were able to apprehend him without incident. A thorough investigation was conducted by Detective Reiter's team. The suspect was well known in the neighborhood. A laundry ticket he was carrying led to finding his current address. They recovered six dangerous firearms from the suspect's residence. One Intratec nine-millimeter semi-automatic handgun, one nine-millimeter semi-automatic, a Ruger handgun, one nine-millimeter Cobra M-11 semi-automatic handgun, one sawed off Browning 12-gauge shotgun, and one 22 caliber revolver. Even though they didn't find the guards' missing weapon, ballistics were able to connect several weapons to the two armored car robberies. The arrest clearly prevented many future robberies and the potential death of innocent people.

Incident Six:

September 25, 1990, at approximately 1830 hours, Detective Reiter met with a confidential informant that had always been reliable._The informant provided information about the whereabouts of a male suspect who was wanted for a pattern of robberies. The address he was given on Park Place had once been a single-family home, but it had been broken up into small rental units.

Michael and his plainclothes unit responded to the Park Place address and were able to apprehend a violent felon known as Tony Davis. Mr. Davis was also being sought as a suspect in a homicide charge.

Detective Reiter conducted a detailed interrogation, during which Mr. Davis insisted he wasn't responsible for the Homicide. He then detailed information about a second perpetrator. Davis claimed he always hit units when no one was at home and didn't carry a gun. He then described several weapons and where they were hidden in the second suspect's residence and vehicle.

Because of the detailed information, Detective Reiter was able to secure two separate warrants. One warrant allowed for a search of the perp's residence and car. The second allowed the arrest of the suspect, Greg Wright. Preliminary checks showed there was no one at home at the suspect's address. Surveillance was established on the suspect's home, which was located within the team's assigned territory. About nine that night, Detective Reiter observed the perpetrator pulling into an empty spot along the street and running into his home. The team staked out the location for the entire night, wanting to see if they might catch the suspect in the process of committing a crime, but he didn't appear. At approximately six am the next morning, Detective Reiter and his unit executed the warrants. The sleepy suspect surrendered without deadly force being necessary. The suspect, Greg Wright, was taken into custody and transported to the 77. The search of the interior of his unit was considered a tremendous success.

Detective Reiter and his team seized a Smith and Wesson nine-millimeter automatic handgun. Two loaded nine-millimeter handguns were found in his vehicle. They also seized a Rycon pathfinder that was used to locate hidden safes within a building. Ballistics were able to prove that the automatic weapons were used in several robberies, as was connected to the homicide.

Detective Reiter demonstrated keen street sense and observation skills in the initial apprehension of Davis. The two dangerous felons were taken off the streets and an extremely dangerous, potentially deadly situation was avoided.

Incident Seven:

In July 1991, while doing a 4 x 12 tour, Detective Reiter and the R.I.P. unit were canvassing the vicinity of Ralph Avenue and Park Place within the confines of the 77th precincts designated territory. They were looking for a male suspect who was wanted for a recent homicide. As the vehicle approached the 400 block of Ralph Avenue, Detective Reiter observed two males engaged in a physical altercation on the sidewalk in front of a housing authority apartment building. As they approached, the two men rolled off the sidewalk into the street. A third male was watching and calling out comments during the altercation. The third male was wearing shorts and a three-quarter length jacket which was rather odd dress for that time of the year. The jacket immediately raised Detective Reiter's suspicion, as he could only think of one reason anyone would wear winter apparel in the middle of the summer heat wave. The perpetrator must be concealing a long weapon underneath his jacket. They slammed on the brakes and identified themselves as the police. The third suspect fled the scene and ran South on Ralph Avenue and turned east on Park Place. Detective Reiter and his partner, Officer Barba, pursued him, and a foot chase ensued. Two additional officers in his team pursued the suspect in their vehicle. Moments later, their vehicle had caught up with the suspect and as they exited the car, he produced a handgun and fired at them. Detective Paul returned fire twice at the suspect, who then removed the sawed-off shotgun from underneath his jacket and threw it over a fence.

The perp continued to evade capture by fleeing down Park Place toward Ralph Avenue. While running, he slipped and fell. Once he regained his feet, he removed his jacket, crossed Ralph against the flow of traffic and fled into 1686 Park Place, a multi-unit semi-connected building, with his handgun in hand. The driver of the vehicle team remained with Detective Paul, who had injured his foot when he exited the vehicle. Detective Reiter and Officer Barba were in hot pursuit and followed the perpetrator into the building, which was a fully occupied multiple dwelling. There were multiple civilians standing in the lobby and hallways outside their units. The two officers held their fire, as neither wanted to risk civilians that might have been caught in the crossfire. The perpetrator escaped out the back exit. By the time they were able to work their way through the crowd, the suspect had vanished. Detective Reiter was able to identify the suspect, and the team went to his home and apprehend him later that night before the end of the shift.

Incident Eight:

In the spring of 1991, Detective Reiter was investigating an arm robbery of a cab driver that had been committed by two unknown males on April 4, 1991. The driver was able to identify one perp as Shamir Pruitt. Detective Reiter and his partner arrested Mr. Pruitt at his home without incident. During their interrogation of the suspect in custody, they learned that a second male, known as Laven, was involved in the robbery. Further investigation found that a man known as Laven was living at 465 Prospect Place in Brooklyn, New York. Detective Reiter and his partner obtained a search and arrest warrant for the suspect. Later that day, the team executed the warrants and arrested Laven, who was later identified as Lloyd Tucker. The evidence recovered in the search warrant was a fully loaded .380 Astra semi-automatic pistol, a sawed-off .22 caliber Marlin rifle, a sawed-off 25/35 Winchester rifle, which was listed as stolen from a weapons locker of the 68th precinct. Lloyd Tucker was arrested and charged with the illegal possession of weapons, possession of stolen police property. He was also identified by the taxi driver and charged with the cab stickup.

After being charged with the two felonies, Tucker asked to speak with Detective Reiter again. Reiter and his squad Sergeant, met with Tucker, who revealed he was interested in obtaining a lesser charge. He sweetened the offer by mentioning he had been an eyewitness to a homicide that occurred on December 3, 1989, on Prospect Place. Reiter was interested. The victim was a 16 teen year old male who'd been shot in the head. The case was unsolved.

Tucker had said it had been committed by a known drug dealer but wanted a guarantee for his information. Based on the information he supplied Detective Reiter, he agreed to present his case to the DA's office. Based on the information he supplied Detective Reiter, the DA agreed to take up his request. After some back and forth, a conditional agreement was made, and Tucker gave out the information.

Tucker said he had seen the hit go down. The 16-year-old victim had been involved in an earlier shooting at the ABC Liquor store in the area. Bugsy, a small-time drug dealer in the Weeksville and Ocean Hill communities. had followed the victim into his building and murdered him. The teenager had an upcoming court case and Bugsy was afraid of him informing the police of the earlier shooting to stay out of jail.

Tucker stated, "I didn't call the police because I didn't want to end up dead. Bugsy is a stone-cold killer." He also said Bugsy was a co-conspirator in the murder of a Washington police officer when he lived there. Tucker was able to make a positive identification of Bugsy through a photo array (that's used in place of a line up). Bugsy who turned out to be John McKoy, a known felon with a long rap sheet. No one had realized he was in the area.

The information generated a buzz around the 77. Later that day, when Detective Reiter's team took to the streets to locate the perp, several other members of the 77th precinct joined the search for McKoy. The large number of officers made it easier to cover the neighborhoods. At approximately 1650 that afternoon, the suspect was located leaving the pizza parlor across from Saint Theresa's school. After a brief foot pursuit, he was apprehended in the parking lot of the fire station around the corner.

Further investigation located his current residence. A search turned up a loaded .380 caliber semi-automatic. Detective Reiter's commander conducted a line up and he was positively identified as the perpetrator of the homicide of the 16-year-old. This was sufficient for them to go before a grand jury. McKoy was charged with Murder II and possession of a deadly weapon. He was indicted and sentenced to twenty years.

After serving only 10 months, McKoy was confirmed as a conspirator in the murder of the Washington police officer. The information obtained through his confession led to the arrest of his co-conspirator. In a single day, Detective Reiter had closed the armed robbery of a cab driver, two homicides, and confiscated four firearms. An outstanding day's work for this Blue Hero. On a personal note, I want to say thank you to this courageous man. It takes incredible bravery and fortitude to return to the job after dealing with a horrifying event. But for him to come back after being shot point blank in the chest and to keep running towards gunfire throughout the rest of his career… it's just stupefying.

CHAPTER IV

Retired NYPD Homicide Detective: Raymond Reuther

This retired grade II detective did 25 years of solid top notch police work. He started his career with the NYC Transit police department in 1992, continuing his work there until 1999. During that time, Raymond was voted the Rookie of the Year in 1995 after his conduct during a violent shootout with an armed perpetrator. He beat out thousands of other cops to receive that prestigious award.

Right after this incident, there was a merger of three departments, and the NYPD, Housing and Transit police departments became one. That's an honor in itself. He was promoted to detective in 1998 and was assigned to the Manhattan North narcotics squad. In 1999, he went to the warrant squad and later was one of the first detectives to be assigned to the Violent Felony squad. From 2003 to 2007, he worked in several top squads in Manhattan. His last stop during his heroic career was with the Manhattan South Homicide squad. He would've been promoted to grade 1 if he hadn't blown out several discs in his back, which required spinal fusion surgery.

(Portions of this chapter were taken from Murder at Sutton Place, Vanity Fair).

Incident One:

One cool fall Saturday night in November 2016, Jimmy Rackover hosted an after-hours party in his apartment at Sutton Place, in Manhattan. apartment. The party lasted long into the night, but by dawn, most of the guests were making their way home. Finally, only four men remained in the apartment with Jimmy. His best friend Larry Dilione had been Jimmys best friend for many years and often crashed there. Max Gemma was his roommate, sharing the apartment. The final man was someone the three friends had never met before he arrived at the party with another friend. Joey Comunale was from Connecticut. No one really knows what caused the altercation. The last guests to leave said every seemed fine when they left. But something happened.

Less than an hour later, Joey Comunale had been violently beaten and stabbed 15 times in the chest. At some point during the assault, he succumbed to his wounds. Three days later, Joey's body was discovered buried in the sand by the police in Oceanport, New Jersey. This would be Ray's last case and one he would never forget. The unusual homicide case made headlines throughout America.

The primary suspect, Jimmy Beaudoin II, was born March 1991, the oldest son of a single parent mom in Fort Lauderdale, Florida. Not a lot is known about his early life, but we can assume that his mother faced many of the usual speed bumps and barriers young unmarried mothers face in the south. He wanted to escape the life he was stuck in. Friends say he was torn between California and New York. He left without disclosing his destination and many didn't find out about his new life in New York City until they heard about the murder on the news. But things didn't go exactly as Jimmy planned. Three years passed. Now broke, and down on his luck, he was working a temp job to earn money for a ticket back to Florida when he met a wealthy Manhattanite, nicknamed the '*Jeweler to the Stars.*' Jeffery Rackover. took a liking to Jimmy and took him under his wing. Jimmy was happy to have Jeffery become a surrogate father to him. Several months later, he legally changed his name to Jimmy Rackover. Rumors flew, many describing Jimmy as Rackover's alleged lover. Later, it would come out that it wasn't a legal adoption, only an emblematic one.

When they'd be out on the town, Jimmy would be introduced as Rackover's long-lost biological son. Eyebrows were raised, as Jimmy was tall and muscular, and Jeffery was the complete opposite. But no one dared put the question into words. Within a matter of a month, the young man had the world by the balls. He now dressed in expensive tailored suits by Savile Row and Gucci. Along with Jeffery, Jimmy spent his summers in the Hamptons, enjoying life among the elite on the eastern shore of Long Island. Most of the time Jimmy could be found living the good life in Manhattan, often hitting the posh nightclubs in the city. Rackover had called in a favor and gotten him a job as a jewelry and fine art insurance broker with Willis, Tower, and Watson. So, what had caused him to throw it all away?

The Medical examiner listed the date of Joey Comunale's death as Sunday, November 13th, 2016. Detective Raymond Reuther was the lead investigator on the case, working out of the Manhattan South Homicide Squad. It was a complex case. During the investigation, he'd obtained multiple leads and folders full of random bits of information to be sorted through. Slowly, the clues came together, building a convoluted story leading up to the victim's untimely demise. Witnesses state that Saturday night on November 12th, 2016, a fight broke out in front the Gilded Lily, a nightclub in the meatpacking district in Manhattan. Most, though intoxicated, are certain the time was around 3:30 am. Several of the clubbers went across the street to a different bar. Joey and a friend went over to speak with three women from New Jersey who'd also been in the club. A few minutes later, two men joined their conversation. Later, the strangers were identified as Larry Dilione and his friend Max.

Evidentially, the women were still in a partying mood and weren't quite ready to call it a night. Larry suggested they continue the party in his friend's nearby penthouse apartment. Woman # 1 stated that Larry was drunk and had mentioned taking some cocaine earlier. Though friends would later state that Larry was normally shy around people. Detective Raymond Reuther believed the drugs and alcohol must have loosened him up, as the three women described him as open and friendly. Everyone had been partying, using drugs, and drinking excessive alcohol. They agreed to go to the penthouse and shared a cab there.

One of the quick-thinking women felt that because they were heading into an unknown apartment in a part of the city she didn't know, she took a photo of Larry and somehow managed to get the last four digits to Larry's social security number. She smartly sent the photo with his name to a few of her friends, just in case something was to happen. The woman relaxed as they pulled up in front of an upper-class apartment building on Sutton Place, The Grand Sutton. The skyscraper spiraled upward from the shadows of the 59th Street bridge and came complete with a uniformed doorman, an elevator operator, roof top deck, landscaped gardens, and floor to ceiling smoked glass windows.

After exiting the elevator, Larry knocked on the apartment door and they were greeted by the host. James Rackover introduced himself to the others. During the party, James kept mentioning how wealthy his father was. At one point, he'd told one woman that his father could clean the ring she had on her finger and make it sparkle like new. Woman #2 said she thought to herself, "Okay guy, we get it. Your dad's a big-time jeweler."

Several hours after their arrival, the three women decided to call it a night and leave together. At the time they left, there was no hint of murderous mayhem to come.

Through the interrogation of the perpetrators, Detective Reuther was able to ascertain that Larry's friend

Max, who also came from an extraordinarily rich family, didn't care for Jimmy. He told the detective, "I always considered him very weird. Something was off about the guy. He was always showing off how expensive the clothes he was wearing were. For some reason, Larry, who came from a well-to-do family, thought Jimmy was an affiliated soul.

I asked Larry, "what's with the attraction to this guy? He didn't have an answer. I guess it was all that flashy bullshit that Jimmy did."

Lab reports from samples taken by Detective Reuther during the investigation showed that both Larry and Jimmy had a history of steroid use. This wasn't surprising, since witness statements claimed Larry had a very violent temper and Jimmy usually displayed a personable and easy-going temperament. Several witnesses stated Larry enjoyed going out to clubs and engaging in fights with other patrons.

Jimmy told Reuther that he hadn't been alone earlier that evening. A woman he was seeing had fallen asleep in his bed, and he had watched an MMA fight on pay preview. "Larry texted me and said he and a few friends wanted to keep parting and asked if they could come over. Jeffery taught me to be generous and to be a good host. I take pride in that. My home is always open to my friends."

Upon further inquiry, he stated that as the night went on; they continued drinking and doing narcotics. None of the guests displayed any hostility towards each other. It was a mellow mood that evening. At one point, Jimmy and Larry began arguing about who was stronger and who could lift more at the gym. Woman #1 said "they were like siblings, first snapping and snarling and then giving each other compliments." She mentioned that there was no threat of violence. However, Larry seemed fixated on his knife. "Larry kept taking out his pocketknife to open beers. He also liked to put coke on the tip of the blade for one of us to snort the cocaine."

As the morning became lit by the sunrise, the woman Jimmy was seeing left the apartment. A short time later, the building's security camera tape showed Larry and Joey outside the building, helping the three women into an Uber. The footage taken from the camera showed the two men going back upstairs to join Max and Jimmy. There was no sign of irritation in either man. However, within the next hour, Joey was severely beaten and lost consciousness. He was then stabbed over a dozen times.

Through the long and, at times, exceedingly difficult investigation, Detective Reuther found out that Max's and Larry versions of the brutal homicide held together. It's hard to tell if that was because they had time to talk and get their stories straight or if they were telling the truth.

Max stated that after the women left, he had fallen asleep on the couch. He didn't know how much time passed between the time he lay down and when he was to be awakened by Larry striking Joey several times. The third punch knocked the victim out.

Later on, during the investigation, Jimmy and Larry told Reuther that Max was innocent and had nothing to do with the killing. This was likely the truth, however Detective Reuther kept plugging away with his questioning. Why the two men killed Joey and the motive for the murder remain unclear. During the days and then weeks of the investigation, they gathered as many pieces of the puzzle as they could. The detectives and the district attorney's office had to leave it up to their own imaginations to piece the crime together into a reasonable case. Rumors flew after the victim's death. The media's coverage didn't help and often made the investigation tougher for Detective Reuther, who remained resilient in his drive to uncover the truth about the murder of Joey Comunale.

One rumor suggested that Joey had rejected Jimmy and Larry's sexual advances.' (Excerpt from Vanity Fair). That Jimmy and Larry made a pass at Joey was dubious, especially since Max was still in the room. 'The women indicated there had been no sign that Joey had a possible sexual interest in a man.' (Excerpt from Vanity Fair). "Nevertheless, the allegation that Jimmy and Larry were clandestine lovers would haunt the investigation and trial, so much that the prosecutors would unsubtly paint the pair as a contemporary rendition of the sociopathic Brandon and Phillip from Alfred Hitchcock's Rope, so psychotically enamored with each other that they were driven to kill for sport." (Submitted into evidence was a text exchanged between Jimmy and Larry where they told each other "I love you.").

As Detective Reuther continued the investigation, the gay sex motive was eventually abandoned. The new theory became a physical altercation over a depleted supply of cocaine. Lab tests verified that all three men had been using the drug that night. A short time after the women left, the elevator cameras caught Jimmy on tape riding up to the 32nd floor where Jeffrey lay sleeping.

Jimmy stated he rifled through the apartment in search of more narcotics. The trip up to his father/ unconfirmed lovers' apartment took several minutes. That time period became a crucial time interval in the investigation. Jimmy's defense attorney argued his client was out of the apartment while the vicious assault had taken place. During the questions by detective Reuther, he said. "I wasn't even there. I never laid a finger on Joey. I didn't get into a fight with him, or anything else, for that matter."

The lead prosecutor asserted that the assault and stabbing couldn't have realistically happened within the disputed time span. That it was a matter of minutes from when Jimmy was entered elevator going up to Jeffery's apartment and when he returned the apartment. Nor could they find a motive for Jimmy to kill him. In the summation, the DA stressed the state didn't need to establish a motive for the victim's murder. The district attorney argued, "There are times that people will commit crimes with no motive at all," she conceded before inventing the argument over narcotics.

The defense responded that the fight was over a bunch of bullshit. No one will ever know because the jury would never hear the argument that the fight was over a bunch of nonsense. Jimmy never testified. Nor did Larry, whose trial was set to begin after the conclusion of Jimmy's, (who would've pleaded the fifth if he was called as a witness.)

This is where the stories differed. Larry's detailed account while being questioned by Detective Reuther, and what he told the court at the pretrial hearings never was to be heard during the actual trial. Larry told Detective Reuther that, "after he and Joey returned to the apartment, they had another drink. That's when Joey's demeanor changed, and he became edgy and belligerent. He instigated me into an argument. I told him James was getting more coke. Calm down. He then slammed his fist on the table." Larry's short, fused temper kicked in and he told Reuther, "I hit him, then I hit him several more times and slammed him into the floor, which knocked him out."

According to Larry, after he'd knocked Joey out, Jimmy, who was in the apartment not up on the 32nd floor, began yelling down at the unconscious victim, "that's what you get for fucking with my boy." Then Jimmy began hitting Joey while he was lying on the floor. He kept on with the vicious assault, slamming his head onto the floor." Larry noticed Joey was having problems breathing. "I heard gurgling noises and saw blood pooling on the living room floor. I was screaming for Jimmy to stop. Max was now clearly awake and observed the bloody mess on the floor. That's when the shit hit the fan and Jimmy began yelling at them both, "I can't go back to prison for this shit.""

Larry said he was as surprised as Max was at Jimmy's statement about going back to jail. That's when Jimmy decided they only had one choice and that was to murder Joey. Larry told investigators, "He said, 'I got to get rid of him, I've got to kill him." Larry maintained that he wanted to call 911 and take responsibility for the fight. "Jimmy refused and continued to strangle Joey." Larry and Max told Detective Reuther and investigators that Jimmy ordered them to strip the victim in order to prevent any blood evidence from leaving the scene. It was unclear if Joey was alive or dead at that point. Larry testified during trial that after he got Max into a bedroom to speak with him privately, he turned around to see a knife being ripped out of Joey's head. (There wasn't any knife wound found in the victim's head at the autopsy.)

During detective Reuther's investigation and questioning of the defendants, Larry had told the investigators, "Joey was dead by the time we dragged him into the bath and put him into the bathtub. Joey's stab wounds were inflicted by Jimmy in frustration over not being able to dismember him." That statement contradicted the state's allegation: the victim was murdered by 15 stab wounds to Joey's chest. Larry told Max to get clean clothes and leave the apartment. Max told Reuther, "I saw Jimmy standing over Joey's limp body in the tub and then he turned and gave me a bone chilling stare as I walked out the door. I was afraid and confused by what had just taken place."

Max contended he was a victim of circumstance. He woke up to a nightmare taking place before his eyes. That night, he certainly was in the wrong place. If he was guilty of anything, it was being too loyal to his friend. Another problem for Max was he just walked right by the building's security officer and never said a word about the murder. He never dialed 911 and continued to lie to investigators during the initial search for Joey Comunale. Whether this was guilt or fear was never proven.

Jimmy denied Larry's version and maintained the victim was dead before his participation in the ugly homicide began. There's no straightforward evidence of who, in fact, stabbed Joey. Or where he had died in the apartment. Neither Investigators nor the DA's office could find out if the stab wounds had killed Joey. There would be clear evidence if any of the wounds were made after death. One thing that the district attorney's office was adamant about was that Jimmy and Larry were in on it together. They without a doubt acted in concert to commit this horrendous homicide.

Jimmy's defense team pointed out the victim had bruises caused by a ring. They pointed out a particular horseshoe ring worn by Larry. The horse ring dent was never clear in any photos. Another questioned if it was Larry's pocketknife that had been used to stab the victim?

How had Jimmy got his hands on Larry's knife? In Jimmy's version, Larry alone killed Joey by beating and then stabbing him to death. He then left Jimmy to handle the aftermath.

The aftereffect of the gruesome murder and the disposal of Joey's corpse would be hard to square with either of their accounts of what actually took place that night. The DA asked the jurors, "why would someone go to such extensive lengths to cover up someone else's crimes?"

Jimmy's lawyer told the court, "Jimmy had a fear of losing his comfortable lifestyle. He knew right away his relationship with Jeffery Rackover was indeed over. The overwhelming evidence in the case left Jimmy no choice but to admit to the coverup of the macabre homicide.

Detective Reuther described the coverup using the two perpetrators' words. Daylight streamed through the living room window. Without sleep, Larry and Jimmy were exhausted. The irreversible horror of the situation had their heading spinning out of control. It was wearing their consciousness down. Larry said that Jimmy took a knife from the kitchen and tried in vain to dismember Joey's body in the bathtub.

(This didn't line up with Larry's version of Jimmy stabbing the victim. He would have no reason to find another knife.) Plan A hadn't worked out the way Jimmy had hoped. The failed attempt to cut Joey's arm off made them switch to Plan B. They needed another way to conceal the dead body and remove it from the building. During the morning and afternoon of the murder, they'd wrapped Joey's body in saran wrap and a bed comforter. Then they scrubbed the entire apartment down with bleach. Afterward, they threw out the victim's bloodied clothing, along with their own and Joey's wallet and a broken gold necklace. They used the building's garbage collection chute. Not a wise choice. Later, the two murderers checked the building for an escape exit that wasn't being monitored by a security camera.

The investigators felt that since the two men had no real connection to Joey, disposing of the body was a temporary buffer and eased their minds. Their thought process was if they could get rid of the body before anyone came looking for him or asking questions about his whereabouts, they'd be able to keep the police off their backs.

As night rolled in, their phones got a barrage of texts and multiple calls from Joey's family, friends, and the Stamford police department. (Detective Reuther was puzzled how the family had the men's phone numbers. His only guess was someone had received the info in a text from one of the three women. It was never detailed in court.)

The search for the missing man was on. Joey's father phoned Larry, only to be told that his son had left the party to buy some cigarettes and never returned to the apartment. The insane thing about that phone call was, at the time of the conversation, Larry was in the apartment standing right next to Joey's corpse.

The two murderers waited for night and would use the cover of darkness to remove their victim's body. Jimmy had borrowed Jeffery's Mercedes Benz and pulled up to the curb that faced his apartment. When the area was clear, Larry shoved Joey's corpse out the apartment window. He ran down the stairs and out the back way. The two men picked his body up and threw it in the trunk. In less than a minute, Joey was out of the apartment and out of sight.

They two men drove thru the Holland Tunnel into New Jersey. They picked a spot that Larry used to frequent as a child. It was a small marshland behind a florist shop. That's where the two defendants dug a shallow grave and buried the victim's body.

Joey's father had also started investigating on his own. The following day, he visited the Grand Sutton, where his son had last been seen. He'd noticed that the janitor of the building was getting ready to throw out the garbage and stopped him from doing so. He notified the police of his fears, and they were able to recover the evidence.

With the recovery of the bloody clothing, the missing person's case became a homicide investigation. Detective Reuther began a search for Larry, who the victim had left with and Jimmy, the resident of the building. Inquires to Jeffrey gave them little information, as he truly didn't know where Jimmy was.

Several days later, detective Reuther noticed Jeffreys' vehicle was a Mercedes Benz and decided to try to use the car's anti-theft module to locate the missing perps. Reuter and the Manhattan South Homicide team, working with the 17th precinct technical team, were able to follow the pings from the various cell towers and trace the perp's path 60 miles to Oceanport, New Jersey. The two men were taken into custody and transported back to New York.

Detective Reuther's extensive experience, tenacious determination to uncover the truth, and solid interview techniques enabled him to catch Larry in multiple confused statements. He finally broke down and gave up the location of Joey's body. The detectives recovered additional damning evidence and were able to crack the case wide open.

Incident Two:

Another famous murder case that Detective Reuther worked on was a homicide in Hell's Kitchen, the murder of 46-year-old community activist Khemria Singh. Singh, a member of Community Board 4, failed to attend the organization's weekly Wednesday meeting. Around noon the next day, concerned friends went to check on him. They headed over to his apartment. Upon arriving, they knocked and noticed the door was unlocked. They called out his name with no response but knew he would never leave his door open in that manner. They discovered Singh dead in his bathtub.

Detective Reuther was on the Homicide team that was assigned to investigate. He found out that Khemria Singh had been seen Tuesday night at a bar in the Hell's Kitchen area with an acquaintance from his neighborhood.

The server remembered he worked for a local Chinese Restaurant. The two men had been drinking for several hours before they left together. The detective obtained a copy of a surveillance video which showed Singh and his alleged killer.

After a brief investigation, during which they showed images taken from the surveillance video around the neighborhood, Detective Reuther was able to identify a Jeffrey Wong. Mr. Wong, a paroled felon, lived a few blocks away from the victim and worked as a delivery man in the neighborhood.

While being questioned for the murder, Wong had told detective Reuther. "He knew the victim from the neighborhood. We often ran into each other at the bar. Tuesday, after drinking together for several hours, we went back to Singh's apartment on 48th Street to snort some cocaine and continue drinking." Under further questioning, Wong stated that at first it was very casual. They sat and talked while they drank. "Then Khemria put on a porno film and excused himself to take a leak. When he came out of the bathroom, he was stark naked, and he began to make sexual advances towards me. I rejected him and tried to leave his apartment. But when I wanted to leave, he took out a knife and prevented me from exiting his residence. I began to retaliate and pushed him backward several times." When detective Reuther finished his questioning, Wong said. "You know what? The guy probably died from falling on to the knife."

Detective Reuther knew there was more to the story that wasn't coming out. He had a copy of the video surveillance from the apartment building. The tape revealed Wong and Singh walking into the victim's apartment together. They showed no animosity on the tape. Something had changed after they arrived in the apartment. It was obvious there had been an altercation between the two men. At some point during the fight, it had changed from fists to blades. No one believed he fell on their own knife... several times.

The city medical examiner's report had contradicted Mr. Wong's statement. It showed the victim had sustained damage to the upper body, face, back, neck and hands. Bruising on the neck proved he had choked the victim. There were multiple contusions, as well as six stab wounds. It contended that Singh had died from a stab wound to the left side of his neck.

During the court trial, the prosecuting Assistant District Attorney Lisa Franchini claimed that after rejecting the victims' advances, "He pushed the victim back and punched the victim repeatedly." She contended that Wong then took the knife from his victim's kitchen and stabbed him six times in his upper torso area and his face. The state closed by saying it didn't satisfy the bloodthirsty killer to plunge a blade multiple times into his victim, he also physically assaulted the Mr. Singh.

Evidence gather by the detective bore out the state's claims. Walls inside the apartment showed blood splatter. There was blood on the bathroom tiles. After the murder, Wong had tried to stage the crime scene and make it look as if Singh had fallen onto the knife. He tried to clean up the blood. He then placed a clear shower curtain over the deceased man's body in the bathtub as if he had grabbed for it while falling. Cops had found a large kitchen knife with streaks of blood on it. Crime scene investigators also found blood on a pair of scissors in the apartment. However, it is believed that the scissors had been used for cutting up a chicken. It is possible Wong may have used the scissors to cut down the shower curtain and left them on the bathroom sink, which still had water running when the police arrived. The police also found a note with Wong's phone number inside his victim's apartment, the same sources said. (CBS2 and The Daily News)

Thanks to the combined efforts of the police and District Attorney, Jeffrey Wong was found guilty of murder in the second degree. He is currently doing tough time in an upstate maximum prison.

Incident Three:

On September 24, 2002, Detective Reuther was working in the Manhattan Violent Felony Squad. He'd received a warrant over the wire from Puerto Rico for a rape of a child at gunpoint. The suspect Jose Concepcion was being held in Manhattan Central Booking in response to the warrant when 911 had happened. The courts were still closed, and the Puerto Rico authorities didn't respond to the notice to pick up the perpetrator when he was being held. The judge released him.

After they'd realized a huge mistake had just occurred, the DA quickly called Detective Reuther's team into action. The hunt was on, and Detective Reuther was assigned to apprehend the violent, deviant sexual predator.

After working the case for days, Detective Reuther was able to ascertain a new address on the perp. Concepcion frequented an apartment building on East 112th Street. Reports said he was dating a single female in apartment 8b, a woman who had two children. During the interview, Detective Reuther explained Concepcion's record to the woman and what the monster was wanted for. She was still hesitant to offer help in his capture. Detective Reuther left her apartment. However, his team stayed in the area in case the suspect returned. Within 15 minutes, the mother called Ray's cell phone. She was crying and pleading with him to come back to her apartment. When he arrived there, she told him that the perpetrator had sexually abused her 10-year-old son on multiple occasions. He'd threatened the child, telling him if he told anyone, he'd kill him and his mother.

The family was transported to the nearest hospital for observation. While he was there, the mother gave Detective Reuther a new cell phone number the defendant was using. Ray immediately called the phone company and explained the severity of the case. He needed the phone pinged to get the perp's last known location. Within minutes, Ray knew Jose spent a lot of time in a certain area through the ping history on his phone. The store was possibly a job location. The problem was the phone company couldn't provide an exact location. The warrant team decided to hit 125th Street in Harlem. Once there, they drove up and down the street until they located the address of the bodega. Detective Reuther sat in his unmarked car and waited for the perp to surface. The wait finally paid off when the suspect came out of a backroom of the bodega. Detective Reuther and his partner, Detective Lane, tacked the perp when he tried to flee the scene. He was arrested and charged with 10 new counts of sexual abuse of the 10-year-old boy.

Detective Reuther's last homicide case and the most significant of his career was Joey Comunale's, Murder at Sutton Place. This brave and steadfast detective helped solve some of the most gruesome murders in Manhattan's history. That being said, he always felt that taking a child

molester off the street was one of his prouder moments. He had a stellar career.

Chapter V
Retired NYPD Detective Joseph Pascone

When I asked Joe if he'd like to be a part of this book and share a few war stories, he answered me with this. "You know it's amazing! We push these horrible yet often gratifying incidents deep down inside. We never let them out to our families or friends. Just to our brothers and sisters in blue. I think we do that, so we can sleep at night without realizing the genuine horrors we've been exposed to."

For me, that's one of the most powerful statements I've ever heard from anyone. It's so true and exact.

Incident One:

Incidents involving children are often the most difficult crimes to investigate and clear. It takes a special person to deal with this type of crime without letting it cloud their mind. Detective Pascone worked in the elite Special Victims Squad. This case involved a janitor who worked at an apartment complex who was sexually assaulting a teenage female tenant.

Detective Pascone knew in his gut that things weren't right with the girl and acted quickly. He did a thorough interview of the victim and took detailed notes of her two-year ordeal.

As Detective Pascone interviewed the victim, he could see the emotional turmoil reflected in her eyes. Like many victims, she was uncomfortable discussing the assault and would offer excuses for the assailant. After several conversations, Detective Pascone was able to build a profile.

The accused assailant had worked at the girl's apartment building for many years. He was trusted by the tenants and his employer. While working in maintenance, he had the run of the place and knew all the little secret areas to hide and be the deviant bastard that he was. No one questioned seeing him in the entering or leaving an apartment. The perp had set his eyes on the teenage girl after she moved into the building. His friendly attitude gained her trust, making it easy to befriend her. He gradually escalated the physical contacts, first with a hand on the shoulder, then a brief hug. After several months and a steady dose of brainwashing, he made his move and kissed her. Being wheedled by his gentle urging and the special attention he gave her, the poor girl was flattered and felt loved. He was offering the attention she wasn't receiving at home. The girl was now programmed and let him continue to touch her in sexual ways and have her touch him in sexual ways.

Eventually, the perpetrator escalated the 'romance' to include sexual intercourse with the teen. This continued, with him gradually increasing the sexual contact over the next two years. The confused young woman didn't realize that the twisted deviate was committing several sexual crimes against her. Soon he was raping and sexually abusing her daily. Some may say that by this time she was of age and knew what she was doing. That's not the case in this situation. She was brainwashed into believing that these types of sexual acts were done by consenting adults.

Detective Pascone began surveilling the building. He quietly questioned select residents of the complex. He also talked to a few of the assailants' coworkers. He finally took aim at the sexual predator and placed him under arrest for his crimes.

He told me, "I was able to get a written confession out of him after hours of grilling him. Then a video confession which ultimately was the stake in his heart. He was convicted of several crimes, which included rape, sodomy, and sexual abuse."

Unlike many officers who were through with the case once the arrest was made, Detective Pascone felt his job wasn't completed until he ensured the victim received counseling. "Years later, she found me and thanked me for returning her life back to her."

Incident Two:

During his career at the NYPD, Detective Pascone worked as part of the Hostage Negotiation Unit. Only the best and most talented detectives work in that honorable unit. One case that stuck in Joe's mind was when he was the lead detective on a hostage call. The caller was a police officer who'd been terminated from the force earlier that year. The unhinged ex-cop felt that his life was over, and he was a disgrace to his family. He was holding his wife and daughter at gunpoint. He wanted out of his life and intended that they were going to come with him as a family.

Detective Pascone worked relentlessly for several

hours, speaking with the ex-police officer. He listened to his problem, his fears, and helped dispel the anger he held inside of him for what had happened that caused his termination. Detective Pascone stuck to the department guidelines which all members of the Hostage Unit must adhere to and worked his magic. After six hours of grueling negotiations, he was able to talk the ex-cop out of his home and convinced him to let the hostages free. Both the wife and daughter were physically unharmed.

It's pretty safe to assume that at the family members needed counseling to help them through the stressful ordeal to which they'd been exposed. I have personally been there as an ex-cop. Yes, at times, I felt depressed and paranoid. Not once did I ever consider hurting my children as a way out of my problems. My personal opinion is that's the act of a coward. Detective Pascones' career was an extremely exciting one and, at times, extremely dangerous. Thank you for your service, brother.

CHAPTER VI - PART ONE

Retired NYPD Police officer: Mike Rutherford

Incident One:

While working out of the 100th precinct in Queens, New York, Officer Rutherford and his partner were assigned to a section of the district that contained a number of bars and nightclubs. They were to move through the various businesses, then observe and break up any conflicts between unruly patrons inside the bar. The commander of the 100th was getting a ton of complaints about one particularly rowdy establishment. Many of the complaints happened during special events. On this specific shift, they'd been assigned to watch a problem bar on Ladies' Night. The club was in an area with a high Polish population, many of which were regularly known for fighting amongst each other. Officer Rutherford parked his patrol car across the street from the bar, and they settled in to observe occupants' activity. If it became necessary, they were ordered to become the NYPD's bouncers for that tour.

Amazingly, it was a quiet night, so Officer Rutherford and his partner decided to take a ride and observe some of the other problem establishments.

While riding toward the next bar on their problem list, Officer Rutherford rolled down his window to get some fresh air. At once, he was assaulted by the unmistakable odor of burning fire. The two officers looked and noticed smoke coming from the roof of residential building up the street. Officer Rutherford and his partner parked the car and called for a fire engine. Officer Rutherford ran towards the burning building. The flames were intense and spreading quickly throughout the upper portion of the structure. Officer Rutherford immediately entered the inferno. He quickly worked his way up the stairs, knocking on doors to awake sleeping tenants. Once he was certain he had alerted all the occupants, he assisted the occupants out of the building, working from the top floor down. His partner was clearing each apartment, making sure no one was missed. Inside one apartment, a few people were drunk and didn't want to leave. Officer Rutherford was able to coax them out to safety. Finally, only one man was left in one of apartments. By this time, the hallways had filled with thick black smoke, making it extremely hard to breathe in and difficult to navigate. Officer Rutherford was able to use force to grab the last occupant. Then, with the help of a firefighter, he was able to carry him out of the burning building. Just as they escaped the conflagration, the dwelling began to collapse. In his own words to me, "I wanted to become a firefighter before I became a police officer, but I'm not too fond of heights." Officer Rutherford and his partner had saved 25 people from the blaze. The local fire captain pulled Officer Rutherford aside and told him. "If you hadn't been here and rescued all those people, they for sure would've perished in that fire tonight."

Blue blood runs deep in thes family & you can bet Gradfather Officer John Rutherford is smiling.

Later in his career, Officer Rutherford transferred to Central Booking in Queens. (Central Booking is the holding cells where defendants wait to appear before a judge for their arraignment). While working that assignment, he'd saved countless defendants from hanging themselves. "I can honestly say that I've saved more lives than I've made collars. I really tried to make a difference by helping people when I could."

It just goes to show you that police officers wear many hats from many professions during their shifts. Officer Rutherford, thank you for your bravery and dedicated service to the citizens of New York City.

CHAPTER VI- PART TWO

Retired NYPD Sergeant: Frank Failla

      Officer Frank Failla spent his first 15 years on the job in one of the toughest commands in Brooklyn. The 77th which has its own legacy, with one of the highest murder rates since the Buddy Boys scandal in the late 80s. Officer Failla was assigned to the command in 1991 and worked there until 2006. While there, he made his own mark by collaring bad guys, often saving the lives of citizens who lived in that area. He was one of a few good cops that helped bring back the 77th's good name and reputation of great policing. Officer Failla would later be promoted to sergeant and serve in that capacity until he was transferred to Chinatown in Manhattan. There, he spent the next three years as a squad boss. In 2009, he would become a squad boss in MTS as an impact leader, retiring in 2012 with 20 years of dedicated service. These are a few of his favorite memories.

Incident One:

While working in the 77th precinct officer Failla was in the Anticrime plainclothes unit. One year, he ranked up eighteen solo gun collars. During his time in Anticrime Frank spearheaded the investigation of a vicious gang member who'd been dealing drugs and scaring the living hell out of the working folks in the area. This gang member had claimed one of the corners as his turf and threatened young and old people, making it an unlivable time for them. That's when Frank had decided to act and start investigating the perp. He was able to get close enough to catch the perp in action, thereby gaining probable cause. It didn't take him long to prove the bastard dirty and bring him to justice. That collar earned Frank a departmental medal.

Incident Two:

In 1995, while he was still in uniform, Officer Failla was sent to Coney Island for a summer detail. Many small mom and pop businesses were located along the main strip or promenade set up along the boardwalk that ran parallel to the ocean. On a hot summer day, as many as a million people would flood the area, often causing extreme congestion on the 80-foot wide, 2.7-mile-long promenade. While walking along the boardwalk, Officer Failla was flagged down by a pedestrian who'd reported there was an unconscious male lying on the promenade. He did an evaluation of the man and determined he was in full cardiac arrest. Officer Failla took over the scene and began performing CPR on the dying man. The victim's wife was hysterical and yelling at him, saying he was doing it wrong and that he didn't know how to perform the procedure. Then her family joined in and began screaming at him that the wife of the dying man knew more about performing CPR than he did. "I find it funny that when there are times of despair and horrible events, that people that haven't received a day of training are all the sudden experts in police procedures. Just to make it clear. ALL police officers are certified in performing CPR and the use of defibrillators." Upon hearing the wife and other people that were screaming instead of trying to help, Officer Failla shouted at the wife. "Knock it off and get down here and begin mouth to mouth while I do the chest compressions." After three rounds of performing CPR, Frank checked the man for a pulse, and it had returned. The victim was breathing on his own when the ambulance arrived. He was transported to Coney Island Hospital.

Incident three:

Ten years later, Frank found himself in the same situation. A man had collapsed outside a theater in Manhattan. If you've ever been in the Theater District, is often called the heart of Midtown and includes Broadway. It also includes recording studios, theatrical agencies, and several television studios. So, you can imagine it can be maniacal. It's an extremely busy area when the plays are in session. Sergeant Failla was driving down West 45th Street, when he saw a man standing in line, waiver and then drop to the sidewalk. He immediately sprang into action. After assessing that the man was in full cardiac arrest, he moved him onto his back and began doing CPR. After several rounds of chest compressions, the man's heart began to pump again. Sergeant Failla remained with him until the ambulance arrived to transport him. Later, he was told the man had made a full recovery. When not saving people's lives, Frank was a proactive police officer, actively promoting physical fitness and mental health.

Incident Four:

During a 4x12 tour, officer Failla and his partner received a radio report of a man with a gun. As they turned the corner to respond to the call, a man fitting the description began running, dodging in and out of pedestrians and around parked vehicles. The two officers leapt out of their patrol car and gave pursuit. The perp kept checking his distance between himself and officer Failla. "Each time he turned to check his position, I slowed. I could've shot at him multiple times, however, I held my fire since the suspect was turning towards another police officer." The officer would have been in danger from the suspect holding the gun, and at risk from a wild shot from the police officer. "The gun will ultimately begin by being pointed in the officer's direction. Which would give the officer every right to fire at the fleeing suspect. That could easily become an immediate threat of deadly danger for the unsuspecting cop moving toward the perp." Officer Failla remained steadfast in his action and held back from opening fire on the armed perpetrator, who wisely tossed the gun after realizing there was no where he could run. Officer Failla apprehended the suspect, and his partner recovered the gun. During the arrest and processing, Frank consulted with the 77th detective squad after they interviewed the perp. It was determined the newly arrested perp was wanted for a triple homicide.

Sergeant Failla is what's known as a well-rounded police officer. Magnificent work Frank. Thank you for your service.

CHAPTER VII PART - ONE

Retired NYPD Police Officer: John Hufnagle

Incident One:

One especially frigid fall night in November 1992, officer Hufnagle was assigned to patrol and was walking a footpost in the Audubon projects. During the 1960s,'

the rising costs of housing was becoming a problem in some areas of Manhattan. To solve the housing shortage, the city began building affordable high-rise apartment communities. New York was more interested in the number of affordable housing units than quality of life for the people living in them. Over the next twenty years, the Housing Authority added additional low-income units along and in proximity to Amsterdam Avenue. The cops that walk these dangerous foot posts in the housing projects are walking solo. When a dangerous situation arises, they have no backup by their side. They must call for help and often have to wait several minutes for backup to arrive. Minutes can feel like days when you're in a life-or-death situation.

Officer Hufnagle's main beat in the late 80s and early 90s was the hardened criminal area of the St. Nicholas Houses, a public housing project in Central Harlem. The St. Nick projects were in the confines of the 32nd precinct, which is fondly nicknamed *Felony Convict Land*. Few cops could say that they walked those hallways alone, on a solo beat, every day and every night. Officer John Hufnagle aka the Huff did. His knowledge of Upper Manhattan was bar- none, the best in the business.

Officer Hufnagle, aka the Huff, knew more about the winding catacombs that made up the thousands of apartments in the Audubon projects better than any cop on the force.

That night, while patrolling the grounds of Audubon projects, a call came over the air about a brutal homicide in the Amsterdam Homes. John was familiar with those projects. The main building was twenty stories tall and held one hundred and sixty-eight apartments. He'd patrolled the grounds many times. He responded to central saying,

"This is post 158. I'll take that call, Central."

He was already moving in that direction when communications responded. "10-4, 158." The building was a good 15 blocks away. And then he had to travel through the building to the unit. The upper levels of the building were often hotbeds of criminal activity. For once, the elevator was working. He stepped out, checking for any visible sign of activity. The hall was empty. That wasn't a good sign. Only the imminent arrival of lots of police would keep everyone inside. Upon reaching the apartment number given in the report, he knocked, with no response. He carefully tried the doorknob, unsurprised that the door was unlocked. Th doorknob turned easily. Because of the nature of the call, the court granted him a license to make a lawful entrance into the apartment.

Officer Hufnagle entered the apartment and did a complete walkthrough of the residence, ensuring the perp had already left the premises. There was a distinct scent of dried blood in the air. The only room he hadn't entered was the couple's bedroom. He slowly opened the door and stepped into a scene from a horror show. His initial instinct was that the murder had had happened a few hours earlier. There were visible signs of blood loss and damage to both victims. Officer Hufnagle checked the bodies for any indication of life, testing their eyes for light reaction and looking for a neck pulse on both victims. He' realized the probability of one of them still being alive was one in a million. The room was a bloody massacre. But he knew the job inside and out and followed the steps, just in case. He was certain they'd been dead for several hours.

After determining the couple was deceased, he carefully made his way through the carnage, back to the hall outside the door. Once there, he made the necessary call to command telling Central of the double homicide.

"Go ahead 158."

"Victims are non-responsive and cold to the touch. Have the housing sergeant and coroner respond to the scene forthwith. Also request Crime Scene be notified ASAP."

It felt life forever before the Crime Scene Unit and the homicide detectives finally arrived and combed through the apartment, bagging and tagging what they thought was evidence in the case. Officer Hufnagle maintained the perimeter and kept the tenants at a distance while they worked. After a few hours, all the detectives, except the Chief of Detectives, had left the crime scene. The CD was so impressed by Officer Hufnagle and how he'd handled the crime scene; he requested that Hufnagle be temporarily assigned to the 34th precinct squad, to aid the detectives on the case.

After the Crime Scene techs had returned to the laboratory, Officer Hufnagle's did a final walk through of the couple's residence. The only room that he'd not investigated was the bathroom. The techs had checked, and everything looked in order there. They had done an initial review and determined the perp hadn't been inside the bathroom. There was no sign of blood, nor any hint that the room had been cleaned after the murder occurred. Officer Hufnagle checked the tub and sink to see if there was any remaining blood to show the perp may've used the sink. John was thinking, "Maybe he'd washed the couple's blood off his hands." Unfortunately, he had no luck there. He couldn't find a speck of blood left on the porcelain. Then he noticed that the lid on the tank was slightly off center. People liked to hide things in toilet tanks, so he checked. Other than a tank cleaner, it was empty. The off-kilter lid bothered him. Everything about the apartment, outside the mess in the bedroom, showed a meticulously clean and organized tenant. She would never have left the top off. He decided to check the tank one more time. By kneeling on the toilet seat, he was able to rest his head and see down between the tank and wall. He spotted something wedged behind the toilet bowl. He yelled out to the Chief, "I got something here boss."

The CD agreed it was unusual and allowed him to remove the tank. Someone had slid a sock between the tank and the wall. It had caught on the raised ridge where the tank attached to the bowl. The CD told him. "Bag the evidence up and rush it downtown. I want the lab boys on this right away. It's a great catch. One that shouldn't have been overlooked. I'll deal with the detectives and crime scene techs when I get back to their command."

That piece of evidence would be the first of its kind in the NYPD's history. The sock had three distinct types of DNA on it. The NYPD lab sent the evidence over to the FBI crime lab to help them on the case. The computers in the laboratory had proven that two DNA samples belonged to the couple, and the third was their nephew's blood. They now had a viable suspect.

"I often wonder how other occupants in a building can't or don't hear a person being stabbed to death or shot. In most cases in drug infested cities, the folks that live there are just too fucking afraid to speak to the police. They fear for their own lives and their families. It's truly a sin that criminals now are in control of our cities and streets. We, as good citizens, must take back our neighborhoods. And we must give back to the police the power to properly enforce the law, so they can protect us from the evil perpetrators of the law."

The Nephew had murdered his aunt and uncle for some unknown reason. More than likely over money. It's unimaginable how someone could be so cold and ruthless to have dinner with family, then afterwards stab two people who'd loved him and more than likely took care of him. Bottom line here is, he's a monster that needs to be behind bars forever. In my book, animals like that don't deserve second chances. John, magnificent work. Thank you for your service.

CHAPTER VII PART- TWO

Retired NYPD Detective: Aura Chacon

Detective Chacon served 21 years with the NYPD. She worked in uniform for 15 years in some of the toughest areas in the Bronx. During that time, she was involved in many violent incidents with combative men and women. One incident that haunts her to this day was an arrest at a housing project in the Bronx, involving one of the trickiest situations an officer could respond to... a violent domestic dispute. You never knew what might happen when a case involves emotions. This case was one of the most serious you could face, a man with a gun and a reported assault on a wife.

Detective Chacon was extremely familiar with the projects because she'd worked for the Housing Police as a P.A.A. for ten years. When it came to dealing with the residents in the housing complexes, she knew all the ins and outs. Her first warning that this wouldn't be a smooth operation was when she recognized the man who opened the apartment. Some men would never accept the idea of a woman wearing a badge. Right away, he was argumentative and confrontational. She knew this call could easily escalate into a huge problem. She's faced men like this before and realized he could start swinging at her without warning. Her intuition was correct, and the fight was on. The perp was excessively big and too strong for her to keep fighting on her own. He gave her a violent shove, and she stepped backward, tripping over something on the cluttered apartment floor. It threw her off balance and she fell, striking her head on a table. The blow knocked her out. The man then smashed his wife in the face and threw her on top of officer Chacon. The wife said he took out his gun. It's unknown if the perpetrator pulled the trigger. If so, it misfired. He left the apartment before her backup arrived. He was later arrested for the assault on officer Chacon and his wife. The police surgeon and the review panel had put her in for three quarters because of the severity of her injuries, but the department denied her. To this day, she's still fighting for it.

Incident One:

Officer Chacon was promoted to detective on February 29th, 2007. After her promotion she was transferred to SVU (Special Victims' Unit) Two years after she joined SVU she caught a case of a male who'd been sodomized with a long shoehorn. The assailant was another male who he'd picked up at a bar. This case was further complicated because the victim was a married man with children and his wife was unaware of his second lifestyle. According to the report, he had mustered up the courage to come clean with her and asked her for a divorce. She had agreed. That night, he went celebrating and met his assailant, who took things a bit too far during their one-night stand. The subject was a foreigner and was visiting New York from outside the United States. With only a name and no address information, the man was almost untraceable. Detective Chacon refused to give up. After an extensive investigation by Detective Chacon, he was finally apprehended and charged with sexual abuse and sodomy.

Incident Two:

A unique case in 2007 involved a city sanitation worker. The sexual predator preyed on women that were intoxicated and couldn't put up a fight or remember what had happened to them. While working at his job, he was able to watch for potential victims, noting women who would drink in bars and walk home alone or leave the bar with different men. Once he spotted a potential victim, he would lie in wait for her to come by on the way home from the bar. Then he would sexually abuse and rape the women while they were half unconscious.

His last victim had put up a tremendous fight and escaped without being raped. She was a cancer survivor and had beaten the disease twice. As soon as she reached safety, she reported the attempted assault.

As soon as she took the report, Detective Chacon realized this could be the serial rapist they had been searching for. The similarities were significant. With the information the victim was able to provide, she went to work. She used a composite image and questioned the store owners and residents in the area but had no luck. Finally, she went back to look around the area of the last attack on 44th Street in Midtown Manhattan. Less than a hundred feet from the scene of the assault, she spotted a security camera that was hidden behind a tree. It belonged to a small business that was closed during the hours of the assault. Upon viewing the recordings, she was able to match the serial rapist to the composite the artist had drawn from the witness description. As a city employee, his image was on file. The victim named him as her assailant, and he was charged with multiple counts of sexual abuse, rape, and attempted rape.

Incident Three:

One of Detective Chacon's' biggest cases was a male who was having deviant sex with a minor. The subject lived on Cherry Street in Downtown Manhattan. This is one of the craziest stories I've heard in a long time. An anonymous tip was called in about a man who was abusing a twelve-year-old girl. According to the report, the man was married to his second wife and lived on the 10th floor of a Cherry Street tenement. His ex-wife lived on the 16th floor of the same building. As if having two women in the same building wasn't enough excitement in his life, the subject was also having an affair with a woman on the 12th floor. Thou it might be considered a sign of insanity, none of that was illegal. However, having sex with the girlfriend's 12-year-old daughter is.

When detective Chacon caught the case, she interviewed all the parties concerned. Finally, the last person she needed interview was the 12-year girl. When she asked what happened between her and the subject, the girl said. "It was consensual, and I sucked his big dick in the hallway and when he came, he told me to spit it out. He didn't want his cum inside me, in case of anyone made allegations against him."

"I made a recording of you saying it was consensual. However, you'll need to show me where you spit it out." Aura had the girl show her where she spit his sperm out on the floor. The evidence was still there, and she collected it and took it to the lab. He was identified through the semen left on the floor. The judge approved the warrant and detective Chacon went to collar him up. The reason for the charges was the 12-year-old female was underage, so there' could be no consensual sexual act between the two parties.

When detective Chacon arrived at his apartment, he was nowhere to be found. The current wife denied knowing his whereabouts, but several days later, she admitted that she'd helped him avoid being arrested and put him on a plane to Puerto Rico.

Detective Chacon and a few detectives of the SVU were on a flight within eight hours. When they'd landed, they were met by the local authorities, who told them they knew where the suspect was and were getting ready to arrest him. The house the perp was hiding in was built like a little fortress. There was a tall block outer fence around an interior house. There were heavy, wrought iron bars covering all the windows. Reinforced heavy metal storm doors covered both doorways. Behind them were metal doors, complete with dead bolts. The entry team had busted open the front gate, but they were having a tough time knocking the front storm door in with their battering ram. Detective Chacon was on the side of the house, watching the back door. She saw a window with an iron grate. There was a slimy, wet black mold streak running down the wall from a leak in the rain gutter above the window. The water wore away the stucco over the window and the frame had rotted away. She took a chance and pulled on the metal grate. The grate came off the window. She could see into the inside of the house. She immediately went to tell the entry team. "Hey, guys, I'm got an accessible window over here. If you keep distracting them by banging on the front door, a couple of us can go through the window. Let's grab this jerk now."

It worked just as she'd hoped. Everyone in the house was watching the front door. The perp was taken into custody and flown back to New York. He was tried and was found guilty of sodomy.

The case detective Chacon worked on very emotional and gritty. Few cops can work in the SUV unit. It takes a special breed to handle cases like the ones they catch every day.

Incident Four:

The Tavares brothers are an American R&B and Soul

music band. Back in the 1970s they had a string of hits. But life wasn't always wonderful for the friends. In 2002, Antone 'Chubby" Tavares' the singer of the band, son Jason, was murdered in Florida during a drug deal that went bad. The killer went on the run and evaded capture for 18 months. Antone was devastated when his son was shot and killed over a twenty-dollar bag of pot. He waited month after month for the Florida police department to catch the killer. Eventually, the murder was shown on the television show America's Most Wanted.

But the perpetrator had made a serious mistake. He went to New York to hide out with his friends and family in the Bronx. Once there, he soon went back to his criminal ways. Not long after the show premiered, he was spotted hanging out on Bryant Avenue in the Bronx. Officer Chacon had him under surveillance but had found nothing they could take to court. Then someone mentioned that he looked a lot like the guy on television, the one that had killed Antone Tavares' son. She immediately pulled the hot sheet and verified the suspect in the murder was standing near a store on Bryant Avenue.

Officer Chacon approached the perp with extreme caution, knowing she might be involved in a violent arrest. It had been eighteen months since the murder in Florida. The suspect didn't know she had recognized him. Officer Chacon was able to apprehend the suspect without a physical altercation, and with no shots being fired.

Antone Tavares told a reporter, "I'll never get my son back, but I know that the guy who has taken him away from me will be locked up for many years, thanks to officer Chacon. I'd like to say thank you for your service and dedication, Detective Chacon."

Later, Mr. Tavares met with officer Chacon in New York and thanked her in person.

CHAPTER VIII

Retired NYPD Detective: Daniel Svenelid

Dan Svenelid was a highly active cop who racked up over 70 medals for bravery. He made well over 700 solo arrests. Many of the arrests he made were for guns and heavy weight narcotic busts. Dan worked in many commands, such as the 40th, Bronx Narcotics, Queens

Narcotics, the 107th squad, and Queens Night watch. Most of his career was in plainclothes.

Every command has its heavy hitters, those few who became well known as the men who made the collars. These pro-active police officers get nicknames on the street. A lot of times these teams get dubbed by their fellow officers the caped crusaders. Detective Svenelid and his partner Eddie Ramirez became known on the streets as Batman and Robin. They were always on prowl for gun collars and narcotic arrests. While working in the 40th precinct, the perps on the street developed a healthy respect for them, knowing they might be the next to suffer their wrath. This didn't make them popular with the criminal element in the 40th district. The two detectives dealt with multiple death threats from the local drug dealers, forcing them to stay on constant alert. Beside the guns and knives, the duo had many objects thrown at them while on duty. Dan once had a block of cobblestone thrown off a rooftop at him. That drug gang only set gasoline to the fire and a short time later, the partners shut down their operation. The lead dealer of that gang was returned to Puerto Rico to serve his sentence. Wonder if he even learned not to throw rocks?

Incident One:

Despite having some of the strongest gun laws in the country, so many guns pass through New York, it is often referred to as the 'Iron Pipeline.' In December 2002, Detective Svenelid spearheaded a gun trafficking investigation that would continue over the next six months. The perpetrators were working in Jamaica Queens. Many people are familiar with the murder of Jason Mizell, also known as Jam Master Jay, who was shot was shot in the head by a masked intruder as he was working in his studio in Jamaica, New York on October 30, 2002. This brought national attention to a steadily growing problem in gun trafficking within the inner city. Officers like Detective Svenelid and his partner Eddie Ramirez were on the front line of the fight.

Detective Svenelid first learned of the illegal activities through a defendant he'd arrested for criminal possession of a firearm. During the arrest processing of that individual, Dan received enough information to contact the Queens District Attorney's office for a warrant. He then had his C.I. registered as an official informant through the Queens DA office. After hammering out all the details, Dan orchestrated a buy operation where his C.I. would introduce an undercover detective as a friend wanting to buy a firearm. During the six-month investigation, in order to gain the gang leaders' trust, the undercover officer had been able to buy seven more firearms. Once enough information had been gathered, a takedown of the organization was planned through the NYPD- ATF task force. The undercover ordered 4 more firearms and federal search and arrest warrants were issued for the takedown. The sting operation went smoothly, and all the defendants had been taken into custody without incident. Once the offenders were in custody, the team hit the apartments where six additional firearms were recovered.

Incident Two:

In New York, officers quickly learn there is no such thing as a minor arrest. During January 2003, the routine detention of an individual exploded into the bust of a huge counterfeit credit card ring. The perp was looking to make a deal. In exchange for a lesser sentence, he began to rat on several people that took part in the swindle. The perp claimed the group would forge credit cards to buy expensive items using stolen information.

During the initial part of the investigation, detective Svenelid learned several members of the Genovese crime family were involved. Surveillance was established for select members of the organization. While conducting surveillance, several members of the group made multiple purchases from department stores. The merchandise was then stored inside residential garages throughout the 110th precinct. Detective Svenelid's C.I. was instructed to make several buys, purchasing merchandise that was stolen by the group using the credit cards. That would ultimately lead to the C.I.s purchase of a counterfeit credit card.

The suspects had a device called a skimmer that would clone the legitimate card and all its critical information. The device was handed out to restaurant employees who would then swipe the person's card and all their information would be downloaded to a computer in another place for the perps to use for fraudulent purchases. Each restaurant worker was compensated with $50.00 dollars for every card they swiped.

The information obtained via the skimmer was then put into a laptop. A sophisticated encoder would place the personal information onto the black magnetic strip of a newly manufactured card. The suspect would then use an embosser to place the individual's name and account number on the front of the card. When completed, the counterfeit cards were of excellent quality and appeared genuine in every detail.

Dan and his team, working with the aid of American

Express, were able to trace the card's activity and develop a solid case against the group of forgers. Detective Svenelid obtained five search warrants for various locations throughout the 110th precinct. Because the criminal activity took place in several states, the team worked with Federal Officers, enlisting the assistance of the Computer Investigation Division to help with the search warrants. The final takedown of the suspects resulted in five arrests for criminal possession of forged instruments, weapons possession, and criminal possession of narcotics. The following contraband was seized during the investigation: three laptop computers with encrypted information on them. Four hundred recently forged credit cards, a magnetic encoder, embossing equipment, hologram machines, lasers, copiers, blank credit cards, discs holding thousands of credit card numbers and corresponding account information, 11 stolen NYPD detective shields, receipts for multiple merchandise purchases and an unspecified amount of cocaine.

After the ring was busted, Detective Svenelid enlisted the help of American Express and Citibank to help trace the origin of the original credit cards to the people who had legally obtained the cards. The owners of the original cards didn't know that they were being used fraudulently. The charges to their accounts were reimbursed.

During the debriefing, several defendants wanted to cut deals. The information they offered enabled Detective Svenelid and his unit to obtain additional search warrants for a smaller credit card ring. Those arrests and seizures resulted in the following contraband being seized. Several skimmers with stolen account information, laptop computers, a loaded firearm, and one pound of marijuana. The estimation of charges on the fraudulent cards was in the hundreds of thousands of dollars. In total, 18 criminals were taken off the street because of a simple snatch and grab arrest.

Incident three:

During the winter of 1997, officer Svenelid was still a uniformed officer working in the 40th Precinct Anti-Crime unit. The 40 Precinct is the southernmost precinct of the Bronx. Officer Svenelid and his partner were canvassing businesses in the vicinity of Brook Avenue and 146th street, searching for five males who'd recently committed an armed robbery. As they were canvassing for witnesses, Dan noticed a suspicious male walking into a bodega. Small grocery stores of this type were common is the Spanish-speaking areas of the neighborhood. This bodega was also a known drug location.

Before exiting the store, the male looked out the glass door, glancing up and down the street very nervously. As soon as he stepped onto the sidewalk, he jogged over to a car that was waiting for him. As soon as he reached the vehicle, Dan and his partner observed another male running to the car. He was also looking around as he ran. The officer realized he was checking to see if there were any police cars in the area. The vehicle quickly pulled out of the parking spot, and the two officers followed. Once the occupants in the car noticed the unmarked vehicle behind them, the driver sped away, driving erratically down Brook Avenue. They were constantly checking to see if they'd lost the unmarked undercover vehicle.

When officer Svenelid finally pulled them over in front of 575 E 140th Street, all hell broke loose. The passenger in the front seat jumped out and started blurting out statements, yelling into the window of the building they had stopped in front of. As officer Svenelid approached the driver, the suspect became excited. He flailed his arms while yelling toward the front of the building. The officers took him into custody, placing him inside the officer's vehicle. The suspect that was driving the vehicle was identified as Mr. Ramos. He was frisked for weapons before being placed on the ground beside the vehicle. Another male in the rear seat of the perp's car was in possession of a marijuana. Inside the vehicle, in clear view of the officers, was a loaded .25 caliber automatic wedged in between the armrest and the driver's seat. All three perpetrators were taken into custody and brought back to the station house for arrest processing. During the vouching process of the vehicle, an additional firearm was recovered. A loaded 9MM which held 17 rounds in the clip and chamber. The driver explained to detective Svenelid that they were in the area looking for 5 males who'd robbed one of their family members.

This was possibly the same 5 males that had committed the armed robbery. That night, Dan and his partner had prevented a revenge war among several gang members.

Incident Four:

On a sweltering hot day in June 2002, Detective Svenelid received information from a confidential informant about two men who were selling firearms within the confines of the 105th Precinct, in the southeastern district of Queens. Dan and his sergeant launched an investigation and were able to identify the suspects. An undercover police officer in his unit was introduced to the subjects through their C.I.. The undercover officer bought a .45-caliber handgun to establish precedent. During the next month, 11 additional firearms were purchased. Once sufficient proof of guilt had been established, Detective Svenelid secured the search and arrest warrants and the team hit their doors the next day. Both subjects were apprehended. Two additional firearms were recovered during the execution of the searches. The subjects were prosecuted under Federal jurisdiction.

In total, this operation took off the street three .45-caliber handguns, one of which was used in a prior shooting, a shotgun, two .38 revolvers, one .357 magnum, one tech-nine automatic, three .380 semi-automatic, a .44 magnum, two .380s, and a sawed-off shotgun. This was all accomplished through great police work and the connection Dan and his partners had with their confidential informants.

Incident Five:

By the end of summer 2003, Detective Svenelid was busy racking up narcotic and gun collars with his Queens Narcotic Unit. MDMA, or methylenedioxymethamphetamine, is a synthetic, psychoactive drug that acts as both a stimulant and psychedelic. It was extremely popular with teens and younger adults as it energized the user, reduced the sense of time passage, and increased skin sensitivity. Unfortunately, it also increased body temperature and could cause strokes or heart attacks. The team had been advised of an individual who was selling bootleg Ecstasy pills in the confines of the 109th precinct. Dan started a short-term investigation into the subject through one of his many confidential informants. He discovered the perp's nickname on the street was Luigi. It seemed that Mr. Luigi liked to carry a large amount of the pills on his person. By doing this, he could deliver the product to his buyers in the matter of minutes when called upon. Dan and his team set up a recon on Linden Place and the Whitestone Expressway access road. That's where they'd been told he would be. Dan and his partner went to the rear of the Whitestone Bowling Alley, just off of the Expressway. They observed two men sitting in a 2001 Honda which had been described to them as Luigi's car. As Dan approached the vehicle, the passenger tried to shove a bag under his seat. Detective Svenelid removed both men from the car and recovered 700 Ecstasy pills and a quantity of marijuana. Both men were charged with B felonies. Criminal possession of a controlled substance.

,

Incident Six:

That summer had been one of detective Svenelid's most productive years in his career. Detective Svenelid and his partner, detective Paul Callahan, were bringing down some heavy hitters in the drug game. The lure of easy money and status draws many people into the world of narcotics sales. Many wannabe drug crews operated on the fringe of organized crime, hoping to slide by under the radar as police concentrated on high-profile criminals. That world is a powerful and dangerous one. In a split second, a police officer's career can be made or come to a screeching halt. The five percenters are a unique breed of officers. Each one of them knows that their lives or careers can be over in the blink of an eye. Yet these men and women keep at it every day they go to work. Detective Svenelid was and always will be a five percenter, the same as all the heroes' I've written about. Now let's get back to Dan Svenelid's story.

Late in the summer of 2003, detective Svenelid launched a short-term investigation of two subjects that were in the selling wholesale amounts of crack cocaine in the confines of the 113ᵗʰ precinct. Once again, detective Svenelid's stable of C.I.s came through for him. This time he'd received information about a man named Mel who had a large quantity of cocaine and would deliver it in a noticeably brief timeframe. Dan's C.I. had already conducted a controlled buy of an eighth of an ounce from Mel that day. A second buy was arranged with an undercover officer. That buy was for a hundred grams of crack. A discussion followed the purchase where the undercover arranged to buy a kilo of crack cocaine. The deal was set to go down later that day. The field team responded to the vicinity of Baisley Pond Park, to set up surveillance prior to the arranged time. They had a clear view of the section of the street where the subject would be waiting. detective Svenelid and his partner went to 157th street and Baisley Boulevard and approached two men named Hood and Christopher. Detective Svenelid ordered the men out of the car they were sitting in and recovered one kilo of crack cocaine. The subjects were placed under arrest without incident.

Incident Seven:

While as a plainclothes police officer in the Anti-Crime Unit out of the 40 Precinct, officer Svenelid was informed by the 40-detective squad that the Southern District U.S. attorney's office was looking for a fugitive named Ernie Rosas. They believed Mr. Rosas was living or working somewhere in the confines of the 40th precinct. The crimes that he was wanted for were extremely serious. He was to be considered armed and dangerous. Officer Svenelid was briefed on the case. The information sustained the premise that the defendant would likely continue to evade capture from the NYPD and the government task force. They'd been unable to apprehend the wanted murderer for several months. His photo was handed out to the Anti-crime unit in hope they would recognize the wanted felon.

Officer Svenelid and the crime boss (Anti-Crime Unit) hit the streets and began the hunt for him. Several hours into the tour, Officer Svenelid spotted a male who fit the description of the murderer standing on the corner of 140th Street and Brooke Avenue. As Officer Svenelid exited the unmarked vehicle to talk to the suspect, he appeared uncomfortable. Expecting him to bolt at any second, Officer Svenelid charged toward the defendant. Rosas fled. Running into a bodega on 140th, he hid behind several stacks of empty cardboard boxes. Officer Svenelid identified himself as a police officer and ordered Rosas to come out. When he didn't move, Svenelid kicked the cluster of boxes down. He then apprehended Rosas without incident. The defendant was wanted for murder in the second degree, conspiracy, racketeering, possession of firearms, and the Rico act.

The act of apprehending such a dangerous person who'd fled and avoided being captured by the government is highly commendable and great police work. Thank you for your service and dedication, Detective Svenelid.

Chapter IX
Retired NYPD Detective: Tim Kennedy

Detective Timothy Kennedy is one of the most highly decorated detectives in the NYPD's history. His courage and bravery are without a doubt, "Second to None." Following in the distinguished footsteps of his father, Sergent Joseph T. Kennedy, detective Kennedy forged a career any other officer would be proud to claim.

During his time on the force, he became a true hunter of the evil men and women that committed violent crimes. Throughout his career, he was a magnet for gun collars, involved in seven shootings, and was the recipient of numerous awards. Tim Kennedy is one of the few NYPD police officers to have been decorated three separate times on Medal Day. Tim is the only detective in the NYPD that has ever been awarded the Medal of Valor (twice) as well as a Combat Cross. Nine certificates of Merit for Outstanding Community Service, The Detective Achievement Award, The Bronx Field Service Area Award, Cop of the Month, and even a Certificate of Perfect Attendance. So, let's get to his amazing stories.

Incident One:

On August 4, 1978, Tim Kennedy was a police officer in the 45 Precinct. He was working the H-I sector (Henry and Ida) with his partner Jimmy during a 4 x 12 tour. Jimmy hadn't picked up his check the day before and grabbed it before roll call was called. He wanted to cash it before the bank closed. They did a quick inventory of their vehicle and headed to the bank on Pelham Bay Station Road. Tim was driving and his partner went into the bank. While Jimmy was at the teller window, a 10-85 (officer needing assistance came over the radio). It was the 45 anti-crime unit calling for backup. Tim hit the horn, letting his partner know something was happening a block away. Jimmy told the teller to hold on to the check, and he'd be back in a few minutes.

Before I continue this story. I'd like to take a moment to explain something. When a cop takes the oath to protect and serve. He also takes a vow never to leave a brother or sister behind or cower away from a physical altercation or a gunfight. A large percent of officers live by that code. Unfortunately, there's that small percent that don't. The decalogue is all a law enforcement officer has and the true officers and agents live by that code. I know I did, and all the officers in this book did as well.

They arrived on the scene at Edison Avenue to find several detectives from the Anti-Crime unit taking cover behind a mailbox. Officer Kennedy asked them, "What's up? What do you have?"

The detective explained that earlier that day, the switchboard operator received a call from Jacobi Hospital. The call stated than a male patient had arrived with a gunshot wound. The operator assigned the investigation to the crime unit.

The Anti-Crime unit detective talked to the victim and discovered the perp's names were Raphael and Richie. The son of the victim had given them their names and their residence as 1915 Edison Avenue. The detectives took it upon themselves to arrest the shooters. The problem was they never notified the dispatcher they were going to the location, and for what reason.

Officer Kennedy asked them, "who's watching the perp's residence?"

They said, "No one."

Officer Kennedy notified central of the situation and asked for backup and ESU (Emergency Service Unit) to respond. Then he joined with several officers, and they surrounded the perp's house. Officer Kennedy and his partner covered the back side of the building. Jimmy climbed into a window while Officer Kennedy covered him. A few seconds later, the next-door neighbor told Tim that the two brothers had gone across the street to their mother's house. Then she said they were heavily armed with several guns.

Officer Kennedy wasn't sure how the two brothers had slipped by the detectives over by the mailbox undetected. He hoped it wasn't because they were more concerned with staying behind the brick mailbox and not paying attention.

When Kennedy couldn't get a hold of his partner, he headed over to the mother's home, expecting he was already there waiting for him. ESU and several officers were already searching the first house. The only cops left to back Tim up was the Anti-Crime unit. Officer Kennedy and officers Ardizone, Ragina, and Reagle walked to the back and Tim observed the curtain to the basement window being closed. In the backyard, they discovered three females sitting on the rear porch of the home. The mother, a daughter and an infant. After an officer escorted the three women to a safe location, officer Kennedy and Officer Ardizone cleared the first floor and the basement. Officer Ragina and Reagle went upstairs to clear the second floor. Tim and Ardizone had finished with the basement and first floor and moved to join the officers upstairs. They knew the perps had to be hiding somewhere on the second floor. As Officer Kennedy approached the stairs leading to the second floor. Ragina and Reagle came running down the stairs and almost knocked Kennedy and Ardizone over. They ran out the front door, leaving the other officers standing and wondering.

Raphael and Richie appeared at the top of the stairs and opened fire on officers Kennedy and Ardizone. Officer Kennedy and Officer Ardizone returned fire. Both officers had fired two shots from their service revolvers. As Tim reloaded the two rounds he'd fired, Ardizone jumped over the railing of the stairs. The two brothers had reappeared at the top of the stairs. One started firing an automatic rifle, and the other shot at Officer Kennedy with a handgun. Kennedy returned fire and shot the brother with the rifle. The other suspect fled back upstairs. Officer Kennedy raced up the stairs and grabbed the rifle on the floor, and kept it trained on the perp he'd just shot. The brother that ran back upstairs barricaded himself in a room and began firing at the cops outside. Tim was seeing a barrage of muzzle flashes from the room. Outside the house, the other cops were returning fire.

When the barrage of bullets had cleared, Officer Kennedy cuffed the brother he'd shot and took him out of the house. He was carrying the perps rifle in his hand. One of the two cops that had almost knocked Officer Kennedy over while running out down the stairs saw him holding the rifle. He bolted down the street.

An Anti-Crime unit detective said to Tim. "Don't shoot him, he's not worth destroying your career over. He's a fucking coward, and now we all know it."

Detective Kennedy's partner, Jimmy, escorted him back to the station house, where he was greeted with applause and a shot of whiskey to calm his nerves. He didn't need the alcohol to calm him down from the shooting. It was for the act of cowardice displayed by the other officers who'd left them in the house with two armed felons. The desk officer was so pissed at Ragina and Reagle for what they'd done to Kennedy and Ardizzone, he was screaming at the top of his lungs. Several officers in the command had to tell him to calm down before the captain came to the command.

The firearms shooting team and riding DA were there to take statements and investigate how many shots had been discharged and from who and where. The firearms team questioned Kennedy about how many rounds he'd fired. They were saying his story was inaccurate. However, he reminded them he'd reloaded the first two rounds he'd fired, replacing them with two more live bullets. The numbers matched, and it was deemed a good shoot. He was cleared by the DA's office and the department.

Reagle later had the nerve later to ask to be included on the writeup for a medal. Kennedy and Ardizzone were awarded the Combat Cross for their bravery.

Incident Two:

During one icy winter tour, detective Kennedy and his partner Lennon were stopped at a red traffic light on East 138th street and Willis Avenue. Later in the book you'll read about Jimmy Lennon and another partner of Tim's, Detective Ralph Friedman. Detective Kennedy told detective Lennon, "There's a stickup going down in the store across the street over there." Lennon looked and just as he said, something out of the norm could be seen happening through the window. A few seconds later, the two males ran out of the store, right in front of their unmarked vehicle. The suspects fled Southbound on Willis Avenue and headed to 136th street. Detective Kennedy and detective Lennon pursued the suspects, weaving in and out of traffic traveling in the opposite direction. The subjects realized they were being followed, abandoned the vehicle, and fled into a building. Lennon ran into the building first, giving hot pursuit with his partner right on his heels. Kennedy slowed long enough to ask one occupant living on the second floor to call 911 and tell them that two plainclothes officers were in pursuit of the two robbery suspects in the building. Mention they are heading towards the roof.

When the officers reached the rooftop, they caught one man and cuffed him up. Tim spotted the second subject fleeing toward a fire escape that was covered in a coat of ice. Tim pointed his snub nose .38 special at him, and the perp laughed. He then started down the fire escape to avoid being caught. Officer Lennon went to chase the second guy, but Detective Kennedy stopped him from doing so, because of the dangerous icy conditions. They took the captured perp down to the street, where several 40th precinct cars had arrived on the scene. One officer advised Detective Kennedy that the second perp had kicked in a second-floor apartment window and was hiding inside. The perp was refusing to come out of the residence. Detective Kennedy and officer Lennon helped secure the inside and outside of the dwelling until ESU arrived on the scene. Minutes later, the front door was breached and ESU took the second perpetrator into custody.

Both subjects were identified by the store owner and charged with armed robbery. While at the location, Tim and his partner had asked one cop what took them so long to arrive at the scene. One cop stated: "The boss said call it off. We have no plainclothes officers in that area." The patrol units then turned their lights and sirens off and slowed down their response time. Another cop pointed out the supervisor who'd called off the job. Tim asked to speak with him away from the others in an alleyway. The supervisor would never make that mistake again.

Incident Three:

During 1979, Officer Kennedy was assigned to the 45th Precinct. A new captain had been assigned to his command. Unfortunately, the new captain didn't have the steel spine as his last commanding officer. The new captain had been approached by the councilman of the neighborhood, which was predominantly Italian. The councilman had an ax to grind with officer Kennedy due to him arresting too many Italians in the area.

After the councilman left, Officer Kennedy was summoned to the new commander's office. Tim snapped him a salute and asked. "What's up Cap?"

"Officer Kennedy, you're not to arrest another Italian that lives in the confines of this precinct. Is that clear?"

Officer Kennedy put in for a mutual transfer to the 52nd precinct where his old boss had been transferred. The new captain tossed the form, saying, "Don't bother, just leave now."

Officer Kennedy wasn't ready to work for someone who wouldn't allow him to do his job. He called his old partner, who'd recently transferred into Warrant Squad. "Jim, I'm bored as shit here. Let's call Deputy Inspector Moran and get reassigned to another command."

Jim agreed. In the matter of days, they were both back as partners and assigned to the 52nd Precinct.

Their first day in the new station house, they were given the A/B/C sector, which was part of the 46th Precinct Anti-Crime Unit. Their first shift was a 4 x 12 tour, but on the way in to work, officer Kennedy's car overheated. His partner knew a service station in the sector.

As the dynamic duo approached the full-service gas station on Jerome Avenue, Kennedy noticed the attendant pumping gas was being robbed by two men armed with guns. One perp held a gun to his head while the other pressed his gun against the attendant's chest. The men noticed the two undercover policemen and fled the scene, heading north against the flow of traffic on Grand Avenue. Office Kennedy notified dispatch of the situation and they pursued the subjects on foot going the wrong way on Grand Avenue. The chase went on for several blocks. When the suspects realized the police were gaining on them, they split up. One hid behind a parked car on the street. The second perpetrator fled into an apartment complex. Officer Kennedy went after the first perp and his partner chased after the second into the apartment building.

I'd just like to let the reader know that this type of situation is by far one of the most dangerous a cop can encounter. Especially when the partners knew both men were armed with firearms.

Officer Kennedy's suspect immediately engaged him into a firefight. He and the suspect exchanged rounds until the perp ran out of ammo. Then Officer Kennedy captured him, and he placed him in cuffs. Tim could hear the rounds being exchanged by his partner and the second suspect in the building. Minutes later, the second perp was down and placed under arrest by Jimmy. After the normal incident investigation, the officers were cleared by the department.

The department felt they were doing their job and put them in for a commendation. The NYPD gave them an exceptional Merit Medal.

That's just a pencil pushing jackass deciding what awards to give out to the real street cops. A total slap in the face to them. They appealed and were later awarded a higher medal... The Honorable Mention Medal.

It's a shame that the bureaucrats in the department have no clue about real police work.

It sickens me to this day. I originally thought I was alone when it came to that bull. But while reading and then bringing these law enforcement stories to life, I realized I wasn't alone in facing the biased decision making of the department. It goes on in a lot of police departments throughout the country. There will always be the police officers that rise through the ranks who are just in it for a paycheck. To the five percenters, it's a way of life and their bodies will always bleed blue. As mine will, until I'm put in the ground.

Incident Four:
Early 1980, Tim Kennedy was working in the 52

Precinct. He was teamed up with another very active cop, Rob Crook, who later would become a first-grade detective. They were working the 12 x 8 tour, also known as the graveyard shift. The night had been rather uneventful, and they parked their radio car to catch up and compare memo books. A few moments later, they'd received a radio run of a 1053 auto accident in front of the main gate of the Bronx Zoo. As they arrived on the scene of the accident, they observed a white Cadillac had slammed into the gate entrance building. The driver was traveling at a high speed on the parkway and heading westbound but ended up in the southbound lane and crashed his vehicle.

A tow truck was already on the scene. The wrecker drivers monitor the police channels through their scanners. More times than not, they beat the cops to the scene of the accident first. Officer Kennedy parked their patrol car in a strategic position to avoid any further accidents. As officer Crook approached the Caddy, the tow truck driver who was assisting the man out of the wreckage saw a gun in the driver's waistband. The tow truck driver made an eye motion towards the man's waistband, which alerted officer Crook.

As officer Kennedy put the RMP in park, he looked into his rearview mirror and observed his partner chasing the driver of the wrecked vehicle. They both were holding revolvers in their hands. Kennedy quickly put the car into gear and made a U-turn and headed westbound onto Pelham Bay Parkway towards the foot pursuit. Intending to pass them to cut off the suspect, he noticed the gun in the perps' hand shift to point toward his partner. He slammed on his brakes, causing the perp to change direction. Officer Kennedy exited the vehicle and a three-way gun battle ensued. There were multiple shots fired between the three men. The subject was finally hit by one of the officer's bullets. Both Kennedy and his partner subdued the injured perpetrator.

During the investigation that followed that morning, it was discovered that several hours earlier, the perpetrator shot and killed a female jogger in Westchester County. He then boarded a train to Downtown Manhattan and shot and killed a parking attendant and stole the now wrecked Cadillac. Tim and his partner were awarded the Honorable Mention Medal. Later that year, they were both awarded The Medal of Valor during the Medal Day Ceremony.

Incident Five:

During 1978, Officer Kennedy was assigned to the 51 stationhouse. His regular partner had court, so Kennedy partnered up with officer Roth for the tour. The roll call sergeant had given them a special assignment for the night. The group, known as the Village People, were performing songs from their latest album in a club near City Island and Orchard Beach. They were to maintain order and keep the peace while the show went on. The boss had instructed them to stay until the very end of the concert.

Patrol vehicles were considered prime targets by local thieves. It was best not to leave them unattended for long. Officer Kennedy was walking across City Island Avenue to check the RMP, when the driver of a white corvette attempted to run him down. Kennedy leapt out of the way of the oncoming vehicle, then raced toward the corvette. As he approached the driver's side window of the vehicle, the driver, Carlos Medina, pointed a loaded gun in his face. Officer Kennedy smashed the gun out of his face and grabbed Medina's arm. A struggle ensued while Tim was attempting to disarm the driver. Officer Roth saw what was happening and rushed to help, running up onto the vehicle, and sliding across the roof. The two officers were able to disarm the perp and take him into custody. While interviewing the suspect, the detectives were able to ascertain the perpetrator had been involved in a recent shooting at an after-hours club. Several people had been shot during that incident. Officer Kennedy and officer Roth were awarded a commendation.

Incident Six:

Sometime during the summer of 1988, Detective Kennedy was assigned to the 40th precinct detective squad. He was driving on the Grand Central Parkway on his way to work around 3:00 pm when he noticed a black auto pulling another vehicle, driven by a young woman, over on the left shoulder of the parkway. Since NYPD officers are told never pull anyone over while they're in the left lane, Kennedy slowed down to make sure he was okay. He figured it must have been a highway cop. Kennedy shot the driver of the black auto a nasty look and drove off.

Seconds later, Detective Kennedy looked into his rearview mirror to discover he was being followed by the black auto. A red light was spinning on the dash of the black vehicle. He motioned to him to pull over, but Kennedy kept driving. He knew something wasn't right about the guy in the black car. Kennedy crossed the Triboro Bridge and exited on 138th street at Willis Avenue. The driver was right up his ass and motioned for him to pull over. Detective Kennedy continued driving towards his command. By then the driver in the black vehicle had his lights and siren on. He spoke over his loudspeaker and ordered Kennedy to follow him to the 40th precinct. Kennedy thought was funny since that was where he was heading anyway. He found a parking spot about 100 yards away from the command on Alexander Avenue.

The driver of the black auto positioned his car behind Kennedys, preventing him from escaping. As detective Kennedy opened his door, the other man was standing there. He grabbed him by his arm and began walking Tim to the 40th stationhouse. As they passed through the doors, other officers in the command, were waving to him, saying hello. Detective Kennedy was wearing a red tee-shirt that said 88th Precinct Anti-Crime Unit. They entered the station house and approached the front desk and the desk officer.

The sergeant looked from the man to detective Kennedy and back to the man who had walked him in. "What do you have here?

The other guy said, "He's under arrest."

Detective Kennedy looked at the desk officer and smiled. Then he reversed the guy and ran his head into the front desk.

"Now, I have an arrest, boss." Tim said. Detective Kennedy knew that something was fishy with the guy. He took the perp up to the squad room and placed him into a holding cell. He ran a check on the suspect and found out he was pulling women over. The he would have them exchange money and sexual favors for not giving them tickets.

Incident Seven:

While working in the robbery squad in the 52nd

precinct, one of detective Kennedy's cases took him to Lower Manhattan during the year of 1984. A lot of the robbery squads work entailed preventing potential crimes by locating soft targets or spotting crimes in progress.

While returning from a victim interview, Detective Kennedy was riding in the rear seat with two other partners from his squad. He was taking in his surroundings in like good cops do, when he spotted a man sneaking around a parking lot, staying down out of site in between cars. A few moments later he observed the male stand and strike a woman. Then he grabbed her purse and flee the scene.

Detective Kennedy had no time to alert his partners of the snatch and grab. He jumped out of the car and began chasing the subject. The foot pursuit didn't last long. Detective Kennedy easily apprehended the perpetrator. The female complainant identified the thief and then she was taken to a hospital. The three detectives transported the perpetrator to the 1st precinct. While Detective Kennedy processed the arrest, the commanding officer advised him he had a task force looking for the guy. He was wanted for numerous robberies. Even when Kennedy was preforming routine interviews of victims, he was always alert and ready to pounce on violent criminals.

Incident Eight:

During the year of 1980, detective Kennedy was told to report for court the next morning for an arrest he'd made months earlier. The next day, he headed down to the Supreme Court building in the Bronx. He met up with the DA handling the case and went over the case. The Ada (Assistant District Attorney) had an attitude with detective Kennedy. They didn't exactly hit it off when working together to convict the defendant. Detective Kennedy spent the day waiting in the ADA's office to be called to testify. The day ended, and he asked the ADA why he hadn't been called to the stand. Traditionally an officer is called early in a trial to allow him to return to his normal duties.

He assured him he'd be first to testify the next morning. The ADA sat in his chair and put his feet onto his desk. Tim looked at his shoes and there were holes in them. He just smiled to himself thinking. "Yeah, you're a real professional lawyer." The entire tour had been wasted when detective Kennedy could've been out in the street making another arrest. That's what really pissed him off. He just wanted to be out on the street doing what he did best. Collaring the shitheads that were committing crimes.

He was told to report to the court again the next day. Again, Kennedy sat in the ADA's office for the entire tour. He asked the ADA, "Why didn't you have me go back to my command and come back when you needed me?"

The ADA replied by saying he was expected to be there in the morning. This went on for three straight tours. On his fourth tour he was told to appear in court again on the case. Officer Kennedy stayed in the street instead. Before doing so, he notified the ADA's secretary that if he was needed, just call his command, and he'd show up to court and testify.

The ADA was angry he didn't follow his order. He notified the District Attorney in charge of Bronx County. Then the DA called the Borough Commander, who in turn called detective Kennedy's commanding officer. The next tour at roll call, Kennedy was advised that a sergeant would be personally driving him down to court for the case. While they drove to court, the sergeant took the Grand Concourse which is in the confines of the 44th Precinct. As they sat waiting at a redlight, detective Kennedy noticed a suspicious vehicle parked off the ramp. Kennedy told the sergeant he wanted to take a quick look. He got out and went to investigate. As he approached the vehicle, he witnessed a male performing a sexual act on a woman who appeared to be fighting him. He ripped the perp out of the car. After a short physical altercation, the perp was subdued and arrested for rape. He instructed the sergeant to take him and the perpetrator to the 44th Precinct. An ambulance took the victim to the hospital.

During the processing of the collar, the commanding officer of the 44th Precinct came down to speak with detective Kennedy. "Detective, did you know this maggot was a serial rapist? I've had a task force looking for this piece of shit for months. Great job detective." The commanding officer of the 44th asked Kennedy if he'd give the collar to the task force.

He agreed on one condition. "Would you call the Bronx DA and advise him that the sergeant and I won't be showing up for court today, due to the arrest?"

"You've got a deal, detective." The C.O. put detective Kennedy in for a Meritorious PD Medal.

It is easy to say that Detective Timothy Kennedy was cut from a cloth that most cops could only dream of. His outstanding bravery and courage are a rarity in the department. Yes, a large percentage of cops go above and beyond the call of duty. But Tim took it to another level. A level that makes ordinary men become living legends. Detective Kennedy, thank you for your dedication and incredible service to the city of New York.

Chapter X

Retired NYPD Sergeant: Michael Loria

Sergeant Loria served in the department for 22 years. He was originally a housing cop, like yours truly, in the best damn department ever. We, as housing cops, would always say. "Housing, the best kept secret." He was a police officer in Harlem and Queens, working in some of the roughest projects in the nation. He then went to Street Crime C.A.G.E. Unit. His colleagues gave him the nickname Big Bird. The name stuck with Mike throughout his career.

After he was promoted to Sergeant, he went to the

73rd precinct in Brooklyn. The 73 is one of the most dangerous commands to work in the NYPD. After that, Sergeant Loria went to PSA 9 in Queens, the Housing Division. That's what they refer to now. Eventually, all three departments merged into one. Now Transit, Housing, and Crime are all divisions of the NYPD. During his career, Sergeant Loria made over 300 solo arrests and assisted in another 4000 arrests. Being the Gang-Anti-Crime and Conditions boss, he's seen his fair share of violent incidents and has helped apprehend thousands of offenders. He was awarded over 30 commendations throughout his career.

Incident One:

While supervisor of the Anti-Crime unit in PSA 9, Sergeant Loria and his team of heavy hitters loved working the 2000 X 0430 tour the best. That tour was easily the most pro-active shift for the team to make arrests.

One summer night around 2am, the sector cars and foot posts had gone home for the night. A call for a male shot came over the air from central. Sergeant Loria and his driver flew over to the scene. When they reached their destination, Loria observed 3 males that displayed gunshot injuries. One was shot in the hand, one in the arm, and the last victim's chest was riddled with bullets. But amazingly, he was still alive. Sergeant Loria called for several buses and gave the description of the suspects to central. Almost immediately, Sergeant Loria was being called on his radio by other members of his unit. "Boss, we're holding two possibles in the Queensbridge houses."

Sergeant Loria knew he couldn't move the third victim because of his extensive wounds. He told the other crime unit to transport the suspects to his location for an identification show up. When the unit arrived, Mike took the two other victims over to the car, where they positively identified the subjects as the shooters. Everything worked out smoothly until the detective squad advised Sergeant Loria, they'd be taking the arrests and processing them. The third victim had died, and that made it a homicide collar.

Incident Two:

One night while the Crime Unit was working in the Queensbridge Houses of New York Housing Authority. The large public housing development comprises 96 buildings. That's more than 3100 apartments with over7000 residents. After Cabrini-Green was demolished, it became the largest housing project in the United States. If you're not familiar with those houses, there's been several movies which featured those projects. They are very, very, violent houses and home to some of the most notorious drug dealers in the country. The team was on the prowl for a collar and spotted an individual who was known to be a real smartass.

This man was a wisecracking, jerk-off drug dealer who always gave them a hard time. He was very good at being a bad guy. That particular night, the team spotted him in the projects and did a quick pass by. They were expecting him to yell at them to incite the other people in the area. But to their amazement, he was silent. A very strange thing for the perp known as the Mouth.

After observing his abnormal behavior, they decided to do another drive. As they approached the previous location, they noticed the perp was walking toward the hill. That's the area in Queensbridge where all the fast-food restaurants and bodegas are located. As they drove closer to the Mouth, he remained strangely silent. Instead of heckling the officers, he walked with his head down and his eyes on the sidewalk. Sergeant Loria and his team decided something was off. They got out and approached him with caution. The Mouth shuffled nervously, he shuffled his feet and shifted his weight, favoring his right side near his waist area. While observing him, one of the cops noticed a bulge in his waistband. They subdued the Mouth and recovered a firearm that was defaced, all the marking were removed. Just by that little change in behavior the team knew the Mouth was up to no good. Great police work.

Incident Three:

Police work isn't always about making big arrests and kicking doors in during search warrants. There are times when a cop will be put to the test to save someone's life, because that particular human being has lost the true meaning of life or the connection with a loved one. They want out and it's up to the first cop on the scene to try and save that individual.

One late summer night sergeant Loria and his team were working in the Jamaica houses, also known as the 40 Houses. The reason being is because of the violent crime conditions. Sergeant Loria observed a female standing on the roof of one of the buildings. The woman was on the outside of the safety fence that surrounded the roof of the housing complex. That particular building was attached to another building. Loria made his way up from the other roof. He could hear the hysterical female screaming on the phone. "I'm going to do it. I swear! I'm going to jump off the roof."

Mike and his team made their way over to her and tried talking to her. But she wasn't hearing them and kept screaming on her phone that she wanted to end it. Since they could only hear one half of the conversation, they had to guess at what point she might break. They moved to her as they could without pushing her into a reaction to their presence. Then something was said by the person on the phone that caused her to drop it. The woman began to lunge toward the edge of the roof, intending to end her life.

Sergeant Loria and his team went into action and jumped, grabbing her as she stepped off the building. They pulled the distraught woman over the fence to safety and transported her to the nearest hospital for evaluation and counseling.

Incident Four:

One of the saddest days of Sergeant Loria 's career was January 21, 1995. He was put on special assignment and placed in the Narcotics unit. His commanding officer at the time was very pleased with the number of collars he had been making. When a request came in for a temporary assignment, his CO put him into the unit. That particular squad was made up of some heavy hitting collar police officers and detectives. They were all street cops and knew their way around the neighborhood. That particular day the team was executing a search warrant in the Astoria Houses. Mike was on the ram and would be crashing through the door when the time was right. Detective Alfred Boesch was working the hydraulic door spreader. Once they were given the go ahead, detective Boesch bent down to work the spreader but collapsed on the floor. He was going into a cardiac arrest. The team rushed him to the hospital where the doctors worked on him for some time. A little while later the doctor advised the team, he'd passed away from a heart attack.

God Bless you Detective Boesch and thank you for your service. R.I.P.

Sergeant Loria would like to thank the great bosses and cops he worked with throughout his career. A special thank you to his FTO Sergeant Couglin and Sergeant Drew who both left us too soon. Thanks to his Gang, Conditions, and Anti-Crime Teams. Thank you for your service and dedication Sergeant Loria.

Chapter XI

Retired NYPD Lieutenant: Gerard Lennon

Lieutenant Lennon served with the department for 25 years and is another proud five percenter. In 1985 he went into the 40th precinct R.I.P. unit (Robbery in Progress) While there he partnered up with none other than the resident wild man Detective Tim Kennedy. Detective Lennon told me during an interview, "Tim Kennedy is the only person I ever called partner."

Detective Lennon had been newly assigned to the

unit and Kennedy took him under his wing and showed him the ropes. He taught him the game as we call it. When you're a collar cop and you become known in the street by the gangbangers and violent criminals, it becomes a game of cat and mouse or good old fashion, cops and robbers. Only the strong survive in the mean streets of the city. Especially in Brooklyn and the Bronx. Detective Lennon was a very pro-active collar cop and loved the action that the street presented to him. Detective Lennon ran into the same brick wall as most heavy hitters do. He'd make a fantastic collar and instead of receiving a medal for it. His Commanding officer would say. "You were doing your job, officer." That's the mind fuck, collar cops go through.

Incident One:

While Lennon was a sergeant in Queens working out of the 114th Precinct, he was involved in some serious arrests. During a day tour all his units were handling jobs that communications had assigned to their sectors. One of the units called for a boss and sergeant Lennon responded to the situation. Some calls are always harder than others, and this was one of those calls. It was a suicide. A male had hung himself in his apartment. While Lennon told central to have the Precinct detective squad respond to the scene, central said, "Are there any units available for a robbery in progress at 23-40 48th street? " Gerry told the operator he'd respond from the suicide.

Central said, "Be advised, sergeant. There are two men with guns at that location."

Lennon and his driver, Officer Frank, drove to the location running lights and sirens. A short distance away, Officer Frank killed the siren and they rolled up to the scene using extreme caution. This was two story, multi-unit building with a central front and rear door. All units faced a central hallway that ran the length of each floor. The unit that was being robbed was on the second floor.

Sergeant Lennon told officer Frank to go to the backyard and cover the rear exit. Lennon took the front door. Once officer Frank was set, he entered the front door and started walking up the stairs, when he heard footsteps running inside the apartment. Sergeant Lennon kicked the door open to find a male victim with his hands and legs bound. The man told Lennon. "Two men with guns. They ran toward the kitchen." Sergeant Lennon observed both suspects in the kitchen and saw they were escaping through a window. As he approached them, he could see they'd been able to squeeze through the window and jump to the lower roof that led to the backyard. He followed.

Officer Frank had his gun trained on both perps. One man still had his gun on him, and the other suspect was holding a meat cleaver. Lennon yelled for them to stop and drop the weapons, or they'd be shot. The first suspect complied and dropped his gun on the rooftop. Sergeant Lennon apprehended him and cuffed the first subject and kicked the gun away from him. The second perpetrator was near the ledge of the roof. Gerry ordered him to stop and put his hands on his head. He then went over to the subject and arrested him without a struggle. He recovered the meat cleaver from the perp's waistband. A dangerous situation was handled professionally and swiftly. Lennon and Frank had prevented the subjects from being shot and them as well.

When they returned to the apartment, they'd discovered five occupants had been tied up during the break in robbery. A second firearm was recovered in the apartment.

One of the victims relayed the horror to sergeant Lennon. "There was a knock on the door. Looked through the peephole and two men were standing in the hallway carrying a box. They said they had a delivery for our apartment. He unlocked the door, and the two men came crashing inside. They ordered us to lay down with our hands behind our backs and tied us up with duct tape. They ransacked our apartment and stole whatever cash and jewelry we had. It seemed that the robbery was a targeted location as they knew one of the occupants owned a business. One of the perpetrators was a member of the Chinese gang, known as the Flying Dragons. He had a large dragon tattoo on his back. The second perp was being initiated into the gang and ordered to carry out the robbery with the other gang member.

Incident Two:

On a Monday evening two males entered a city bus at 51st street and Broadway in Queens New York. After they boarded the coach, they produced guns and proceeded to rob all the passengers. A total of eighteen men and women were robbed at gunpoint. The men told the bus driver to pull over when they'd finished taking the last victim's belongings. They quickly exited the vehicle and fled into the Woodside housing projects. By the time the police arrived the suspects were long gone.

Tuesday evening detective Lennon and the 114th Precinct Anti-Crime team were doing a 4x12 tour and met up with the new commanding officer. The captain's orders for the unit were to concentrate on the Woodside

Houses and obtain any information available on the bus robbery. The subjects had fled into those projects for one reason. That was home to them and there were plenty of buildings to hide out in. Detective Lennon had his unit flooded the area and ruffled as many feathers as possible in an effort to get any good intelligence on the perpetrator's.

Detective Lennon and his partner hit the streets and headed to the Woodside complex. Just as they pulled into traffic, a call came over the air that an armed robbery and violent assault had taken place on Steinway Street. Apparently, a group of males had committed the robbery and fled in a blue Ford Taurus.

As detective Lennon drove up to the Woodside Houses at 48th street and Broadway, Lennon observed 4 males in a Mercedes Benz sitting at the light, opposite him and his partner. The driver of the Mercedes seemed nervous and unfamiliar with the car. It was also a very expensive vehicle for that area. Detective Lennon told his partner to follow them, but not do anything to spook them. At 41st street the driver committed a driving violation. That gave them probable cause to pull them over. As the Mercedes pulled over to the curb, Lennon saw the passenger lean forward and put something under the seat.

Detective Lennon called for backup. "No lights or sirens guys. These men may be armed. Proceed with extreme caution."

"10-4 boss." As the other patrol cars arrived Detective Lennon got out and removed the four males from the vehicle. One they were secured, he looked under the seat where the passenger had placed the object. He recovered a loaded .38 caliber revolver. Further search of the vehicle produced two additional loaded firearms, a ski mask, and an expensive Rolex watch.

During the processing of the collars, an officer noticed one of the guns, a .380 automatic had fresh blood on it. The watch was identified as property taken during the earlier Steinway Street robbery.

The 114th Rip Unit assisted with the lineups and the males were all positively identified by the victim. During the interviews one of the subjects said he wanted to talk. Experience had taught Lennon that he wanted to trade info for a deal. The perp said, "Two of the guys in the holding cell are the dudes that stuck up that bus yesterday."

Instead of calling in the DA, Detective Lennon and the R.I.P. unit brought in the eighteen bus victims. They did a photo lineup at the station house and the victims identified the two men who had robbed them. Lennon and his team had closed out nineteen robberies that night.

Incident Three:

During a summer shift sergeant Lennon and his driver Mike answered a radio run of an armed robbery in progress on Crescent Street and 30th Avenue. When they arrived at the scene, two males informed them that they'd just been robbed by a male who was wearing all orange. He took their cash and got into a taxi and headed down 21st street.

Sergeant Lennon advised central of what had taken place and gave out the description of the wanted felon. Then sergeant Lennon and his partner began to canvass the area for the perp. They headed up to 8th street and Astoria Boulevard. While canvassing, sergeant Lennon spotted a male in orange that fit the description speaking with another male in a building courtyard on Astoria Boulevard. He advised communications he had eyes on a subject that fit the description. As Lennon approached the man in orange, the perp removed a firearm from his pocket and fled into a building in the courtyard. Sergeant Lennon gave chase and a foot pursuit ensued. As Lennon entered the building, the subject saw him and fled up the hallway stairs. At the top of the stairs the perp stopped and pointed his weapon at sergeant Lennon who was approximately five feet away from the felon. Instead of firing at the perp, he lowered his shoulder and jack knifed the bastard into the wall, knocking him backwards down the stairs.

The perpetrator got up off the floor and ran straight into Lennon's partner, who was watching the back exit. He slammed his gun into the officer's chest, forcing him backward. The officer pointed his weapon into the perp's chest and fired, but his gun misfired. The startled perp fled, and the officer cleared the misfired round from his chamber. Lennon called for backup and the subject was quickly identified by his orange outfit. He was apprehended without further incident. The man in orange had thrown his revolver onto the ground, but it was recovered. The gun was still fully loaded. The perp was identified as the person who'd committed the robbery. When they got back to the station house and conducted the interview, he tried to plead mistaken identity. It didn't get much traction, beside the bright orange outfit, the felon still had the outline of Mike's gun on his chest.

Incident Four:

In the early to mid-90's New York City construction sites were plagued by groups known as coalitions. These roving bands of people traveled in vans and cars to construction sites throughout the city demanding jobs for their members, using any means necessary to convince the company to hire the coalition members. The unqualified group would often threaten a foreman and the construction workers with physical force, sometimes with firearms. Many of the job sites would give in to the threats and hire two or three men to keep the unruly group at bay. Other coalitions used less physical threats, such as threatening to report dozens of safety violations against builders and force the job to be interrupted and possibly shut down. The foreman or Shop Stewart had no choice but to keep the peace with the coalition, hiring the men for no show jobs. This type of extortion could cost a builder thousands of dollars weekly. The IRS even began accepting images of cancelled checks with the word extortion listed as a memo. Many problems arose when more than one coalition showed up at the same job site. That's when the NYPD got involved.

In the confines of the 114th Precinct On 21st street and Broadway there was a large construction site building a city school. Around 11 am central received a job call to that location. She assigned the radio run to the Anti-Crime Unit. Sergeant Lennon and his driver said they'd respond. The foreman told Lennon that a large group came onto the grounds demanding jobs and threatened him and one of the members had a gun. They left quickly when they heard the police coming.

The following morning sergeant Lennon was sent back to the work zone due to a large group of men demanding jobs. There were several patrol units on the scene when he arrived. The construction workers were in a faceoff with the coalition group. There were ten uniform police officers standing in-between them. The commanding officer of the 114th Precinct was also on site and somehow brokered a deal between the foreman and the leader of the group. The men from the coalition got back into their van and left the front passenger seat open for their leader, who was still speaking with 114th Precinct Captain.

The original sector car that had been assigned to the job placed a parking summons onto the van. Sergeant Lennon asked the officer if they were taking any further action. They stated they were done, and the van could leave the area. Lennon approached his boss who was still talking to the coalition leader. "Boss, I think we should give the van a toss. There was a member with a gun yesterday when we responded to the scene. But they took off when we arrived."

"We're almost done here sergeant. It would probably

be better to let them leave." He never told Lennon not to search the van.

Sergeant Lennon called his driver over to the van and they began a series of stop, question, and frisks on the members in the first van. After they were done tossing the men in the vehicle, Lennon instructed his driver to stand by the van's side door and not let any of them back into the vehicle until he was done looking around it.

Sergeant Lennon began his search in the front of the van. He looked under the front seats and observed two 9MM handguns which were fully loaded. That discovery allowed him to call the other officers at the location to assist him. He placed each member that was in the van under arrest. He then told another officer to hold the male that was talking to his captain. The officer searched the leader and recovered a loaded 22 caliber revolver from his waistband. There was an additional van on the job site and several males occupying it. They were removed from the van. Seargent Lennon had heard several objects being dropped in that vehicle. Inside that van there were four more loaded guns. A total of seven firearms were seized and 18 coalition members were arrested. His commanding officer called him into his office and gave him a big thank you. It was a long day for sergeant Lennon and his driver. Processing 18 subjects takes a very long time.

Sergeant Lennon was the type of cop you wanted by your side in the heat of battle. He told me that Tim Kennedy was the best cop he'd ever worked with on the streets. Gerry, I'd like to thank you for your service and dedication to the city of New York.

Chapter XII

Retired Frankfort, Kentucky, Police Officer: Brooke Wayne Christopher

Brooke's career as a cop was nothing short of incredible. Brooke Christopher would like to dedicate his chapter to all of the police officers who've gone through something similar to his incident. He'd always wanted to be a police officer. Growing up on a farm on the outskirts of Frankfort Kentucky, the state and local law enforcement were respected and a profession to aspire to. So, after A two-year hitch in the Navy, he came back to Frankfort and began employment with the Frankfort Police Department as a dispatcher because he wasn't 21 yet. Brooke loved working for the department and couldn't wait until he turned the age to pin the shield onto his chest. At 21 he was hired as a full-time police officer and went to the academy. When he graduated, he was also sworn in. It was the happiest day of his life. Brooke Christopher dearly loved all aspects of law enforcement and hoped to have a long career.

Incident One:

On November 15, 1985, officer Christopher was in his sixth year with the department. The day began kind of chilly and he had that Friday night off. Around 11 pm, Brooke decided to go to a local hangout in Frankfort called the Cave Disco. He arrived and spent about three hours in the Cave, talking to people. He drank one beer and at closing set the bottle down. It was still half full. Officer Christopher explained to me. "I'm just not a big drinker."

Around 2:00 in the morning, he walked out to the parking lot to get into his vehicle and go home. Behind him, he heard someone shout fight! Christopher turned and went back to break it up. As he approached, someone said he's got a gun. Officer Christopher knew he may have stumbled upon a serious situation. Upon his arrival, he saw it certainly was just that, a chaotic problem.

The perpetrator had someone in a headlock, with a .45-caliber automatic press against his head. As soon as he saw there was a gunman holding a hostage, officer

Christopher drew his off duty .38 revolver and identified himself as a Frankfort police officer. He then ordered him to drop his gun and release the hostage. The subject continued to wrestle with the hostage and started to wave his gun around. There were people everywhere, so Brooke shouted for them to get back and call the police. "Tell them I need backup." A lot of people were still in his backdrop, and in the line of fire. He was forced to hold his fire since he couldn't risk injuring any of them. He literally pleaded and begged for the perp to drop his weapon. Officer Christopher was trying to buy some time in case he had to use deadly force on the intoxicated perp.

Finally, the man released the hostage but was still waving and pointing his gun around. There were still too many people in the parking lot for officer Christopher to take a shot without the risk of hitting someone. He tried to get between the subject and some people. The entire time, Christopher was pleading with him to drop his gun and they could work it out. He finally was able to separate himself and the armed perp away from the crowd. Without warning, the perpetrator turned and pointed the gun at him. Time slowed. Officer Christopher thought, "Here it comes. He is going to shoot and kill me." He let loose with his .38 revolver and fired three shots.

One shot hit the armed man in the abdomen. He remembered the perp saying. "You got me." Then he fell to the ground. Officer Christopher approached him with his weapon still covering him. When he got up close to the perp, he raised his weapon and said, "You motherfucker!" Christopher grabbed a hold of the man's weapon and tried to take it from him. Several times during the struggle, the weapon was pointed at him. He'd finally succeeded in getting his gun away from the perp and then screamed for an ambulance.

At 1 pm the next day, Officer Christopher arrived with his attorney at police headquarters. His Attorney took over and was very thorough, always keeping Officer Christopher's best interest in mind. At no time during this investigation did the department ever say, "You did the right thing and we're going to stand behind you." Officer Christopher tried to pry anything out of the brass that could be helpful in his case. He was being stonewalled by his own people. The department seemed disinclined to commit one way or another. During that time of abandonment by the department, Christopher thought it would cost him his career and sanity.

The investigation was completed, and a coroner's

inquest was held in January of 86. Officer Christopher was terrified as he testified before them. He did so in full uniform and presented himself very professionally. At the end of the inquest, all the jurors voted his actions were justified, and that he'd acted in the line of duty. When he returned to work, everything was totally different. Life was so much more serious after the hearing. He noticed that the public he served and protected began to distance themselves from him. He kept to himself and descended into the depression that has haunted him since then.

Seeing how everyone in the small town reacted, Officer Christopher wondered what would happen if, in the future, he had to use deadly force again? Would the police officers and the supervisors have his back if the bullets were flying in a shootout? Or would he be shot in the line of duty because he was shunned by the department?

Christopher considered himself a well-trained and seasoned officer. He went through the rest of the year on rote training from the past. There were a couple of times when things got very dicey. One was an alarm drop at the savings and loan bank when one cleaner wouldn't show his hands. The other was a domestic call where both the wife and husband ganged up on him and they crashed through a glass coffee table. Both of them went to jail. Exactly one year to the day after the shooting, he was working a day shift and was called into the Sheriff's office. When he arrived, the sheriff tossed a document at officer Christopher. He just sat in his chair, never saying a word to him. Brooke Christopher was being sued personally for wrongful death. He found out later the sheriff was related by marriage to the person he'd shot.

At the time, for the life of him, he couldn't figure out

why this lawsuit didn't include the city? It was ruled an *in the line of duty shooting*, even though he was off that night. You're in your jurisdiction as a police officer 24/7. If someone is in danger, you must take action, on or off duty. That's the oath every police officer takes.

When Brooke contacted his Chief, he advised him he'd check on it and get back to him. That began a long, agonizing wait for Brooke to get an answer. Three weeks went by, and he found out the city had hired an attorney. The attorney hired a Lexington Police detective to prepare for trial. Brooke met with the attorney at Police HQ, and the first words out of his mouth was that the city was his first priority. It was a crushing blow to him, considering the pressure he was already under.

After a couple of weeks, the investigator from Lexington came down and did a thorough job of going over the shooting scene and evidence. Brooke had another meeting with the attorney. He told him he was to draft a letter to the opposing attorneys. In no uncertain terms, if they didn't drop the lawsuit in one week, then officer Christopher would never ever give up counter suing them. He told the attorney if he didn't do exactly what he demanded, he'd file a complaint with the Bar Association. The lawyer stomped out of police headquarters and three days later, the suit against Brooke was dropped. He was relieved the legal part was over, but his life spiraled down with bouts of depression and PTSD. It was so bad he would wake up screaming from nightmares. He often suffered flashbacks while at work.

He was able to maintain a facade with the department, and he even made good evaluations. Finally, the pressure became too much, and Officer Christopher went into headquarters and privately met with his Boss. He broke down crying and told him. "I just can't take it anymore."

As he started to remove his gun belt and badge, and his lieutenant said, "Don't resign. Take some time off and get some help."

The department set him up with a Lexington police Chaplin, who did absolutely nothing for him. That's when he got help from a Lexington Doctor. The doctor said he'd gone too far without getting treatment and should leave law enforcement. "Brooke, it's time to leave active duty and get out on disability retirement." Brooke didn't know there was such a thing as disability retirement until he'd read the state law on it. He got a letter from the Doctor putting him on permanent sick leave pending retirement. His career was over.

After a month off, Brooke spiraled even deeper into depression. He became very suicidal. He quit eating and stayed alone. Finally, the doctor said that he had to be hospitalized. He checked into the hospital ward the next day. It took a month for them to stabilize him before they sent him home. Brooke went to his father's farm and didn't leave there for about a month. He stayed off for almost a year until he had exhausted all of his vacation, comp time and sick leave and then the city stopped paying him. Brooke thought he was going to lose his house. He had to sell one of his cars and boat to help pay his medical expenses. He contacted his attorney, whose help he's still grateful for, to this day. Then he went down to city hall. His lawyer ripped them apart. A couple of months went by, and a new city government came in. One of the first things they did was to grant his disability retirement. Brook Christopher was the first officer in the department's history to receive disability retirement. At a young age, Brooke's life was in absolute shambles.

He tried to pick up the pieces of his life afterwards but had problems concentrating when attending college. It took him three years to get an associate degree in liberal arts. He went back to work for the state. As soon as he walked in the door the rumors about him as a police officer started flying. People were skittish and distant towards him, and he could feel the resentment. He worked there for 5 years, had a blowup and breakdown at work, and finally just left. The ex-hero cop started mowing lawns. It allowed him to work outside alone most of the time. He even went back to work for the state after fifteen years of operating a successful landscaping business.

It was a quasi-law enforcement state agency. After about 3 years, his supervisor told him. "Oh, by the way. I talked to the Frankfort police chief, and he said, 'If Brooke hadn't listened to some of the older officers, he'd still be in the department." Brooke just about fell through the floor when he heard this. He began a downward spiral that ended with him literally walking off the job and never returning.

Brooke became very suicidal again and had to be hospitalized at the VA for about a week before being released. Afterward, the VA and social security administration granted him full disability. The economic situation improved, but the depression didn't. During 2011, Brooke suffered a massive heart attack and almost died. He still has bad days with depression and the pressures of living. Brooke told me while I interviewed him. "It seems no one but other police officers who've been through these unfortunate situations can understand what I've gone through. Some officers have it much worse than me and my heart goes out to them. In the end, I'm a survivor. If I had it to do all over again, I'd do whatever it took to ensure the safety of the citizens I was sworn to serve and protect. Even knowing that I'd go through this hell for the rest of my life. My thanks to the author and friend and brother Pete Thron for letting me share my story. To all the lawmen and law women out there; may God always be with each and every one of you."

Officer Brooke Wayne Christopher, you're a True-Blue-Warrior. Thank you for your dedication and service to the people of Frankfort, Kentucky.

Chapter XIII

Retired NYPD Sergeant: Jay Cousin

I had the distinct pleasure of working in the same command as Jay. He was true blue to the end. The kind of police officer I wanted next to me when the shit hit the fan. Jay always had my back, and the back of all the other cops that he served with. I wasn't on the job when he'd made sergeant. But I sure wish I was. I would've given my right arm to be in his squad. He knew how to deal with the perps and had chosen the most dangerous project in

145

the command to work in. Mind you, he patrolled that project alone. I knew many police officers who begged not to be put on a foot post in the Polo Grounds. I called that area the world of convicts. Violence was the endgame in those project grounds. Shooting, drug deals, robberies, rapists, and murders roamed the grounds and the floors of the buildings. Sergeant Cousin had balls of steel.

Incident One:

It must have been in the teens that night. It was the beginning of February 1986, and the city was frozen solid. Just ice and solid snow, but clear as a bell. You could breathe and see all the frost in the air. It was a few hours after midnight. Those tours were always easy to work and find collars. The only guys out there were the ones up to no good. It was basically us and them, quiet, but you always had the feeling something could pop off at any time. There's nothing like slowly rolling down an empty, frigid block in the middle of winter. All you hear and feel is the crunch of the RMP tires on icy pavement and eyes peering at you from shadowy alleys and darkened doorways. They tell you in the academy to be sympathetic to the *Us vs. Them* syndrome. But 'it is what it is', as they say and like most of the stuff you learn in the Academy. It's just academic.

At 2am in the morning in Harlem, in the middle of winter, it is *Us vs. Them*. That's the reality, despite what you may hear from the news. Jeff's partner, Gordo, was driving and he handled an RMP like a Daytona race car driver. Sergeant Cousin loved working with Gordo. They made an outstanding team on the streets of Harlem. Their personalities were a good fit, and the number one thing is they always had each other's six. The two of them knew when to kid around and when to work. They could read each other pretty well. The good times never lasted long, and sure enough, there was an armed cab robbery on 132nd Street and Madison. Right next to the stinking Lincoln Houses. The perp was on foot and several units were involved, including Cousin and Gordo. The perp ran across 132nd street and Park Avenue. And of course, what do perps do in the middle of winter?

They jump in the Harlem River.

What the hell! Well, there he was now, about 10 feet down along the bulkhead. The two officers could see him bobbing up and down like a cork. He wouldn't last long in that freezing water with all his heavy clothes on. Cousin and his partner had to forget the drowning man is a perp who had just robbed a cabbie at gunpoint. Knowing that it was only a matter of minutes before the icy water brought the man's temperature down to the point of lost consciousness, they switched into two compassionate, lifesaving machines. The perp was going under and coming back up, gasping for air. If they'd jumped in with him, both of the police officers would become two more poor souls who needed to be rescued.

A couple of guys from the 25th precinct produce a nylon rope from God knows where and drop it down to the perp. His hands were so cold he was having a difficult time grabbing it. He was built like a brick shithouse and weighed a ton. You could tell from his cries; he was desperate to get out of that deadly icebox. They managed to get him halfway up, but he lost his grip and fell back and slipped under the water again. He was bobbing up again. One cop threw him down a pair of leather gloves. Somehow, he got the gloves on and swam to a ledge in the middle of the wall. He was hanging on, but it was only a matter of time before his body started shutting down. The cop with the rope made a loop, and they tried again. This time he got the loop under his arms and the gloves helped him to get another grip. It took several officers, but together they hauled his sorry ass out of the river and away from an icy grave.

The perp was completely exhausted and half frozen. He was easy to cuff and ready to get into the bus (ambulance) for the ride to a warm hospital bed. They took him to the old North General Hospital. Where he was under guard, of course. Good collar, good save and all is well. No one was seriously hurt. But that's the NYPD. Nothing comes easy.

The next night was colder than the previous night and Cousin and Gordo were hunched down in their RMP, hoping for a quiet night. That wasn't going to happen.

Two in the morning must be the agreed upon time when all hell can break loose in the neighborhood. The cop guarding their newly rescued river perp was screaming into his radio. "He's got my gun! I'm at North General Hospital". Cousin and Gordo go tearing over to North General and run into the hospital trying to find the cop. Gunshots were popping off, but they knew they needed to find their brother in blue. Officer Cousin found the 25-Precinct cop on the 2nd floor, bleeding from a head wound. He was dazed and scared. The front half of his holster was lying on the floor. The leather stitching was all shredded. His gun belt was turned around on his body. His .38 is missing in action.

They checked the room and of course, the perp wasn't lying in the bed. It was easy to see how he'd escaped; the bed rail was missing. Apparently, he was carrying it with him. Jay and Gordo didn't know where the perp was, but a couple more shots were heard, so things were still out of control. Clearly more units had arrived on the scene. A few cops tended to the fallen officer, getting him to safety and under a doctor's care. He wasn't shot but had been smashed over the head. Cousin and his partner located the perp in the hospital basement. He was holding hostages. That was bad enough; he was also held up in a room where oxygen tanks were stored and threatened to blow a top gauge off one of the tanks. Not exactly a wonderful situation, but not as bad as it sounds. When you have a perp barricaded, it becomes a wait and see situation. The ESU Hostage negotiation unit was called in and it became a process of waiting until the perp acts. Your options are limited when innocent hostages are involved. The most favorable outcome is he would get tired and give up without hurting the hostages. That's exactly what had happened. The perp gave up after a few hours, and the hostages were released. Again, no one was DOA.

Gordo and Cousin interviewed the injured cop who was still scared out of his wits. Apparently, the prisoner they nicknamed the river monster perp was handcuffed to the bed rail. He had been working his bed rail, back and forth all day and evening and had finally broken it loose. He waited until the getting was good and jumped out of his bed, carrying the bedrail with him. When the officer noticed the irritating click clack noise had stopped, he got up check, and the prisoner brought that bedrail down over the officer's head, knocking him to the floor. He then reached down and grabbed the grip of the officer's 38 revolver and ripped it down and out, literally tearing the stitching out of the holster. The guy had some strength, and it wasn't a defective holster. He then pointed the gun at the officer's head and spoke. "How do you like it now?"

That's gratitude for you. No good deed goes unpunished. Thankfully for the cop, he didn't pull the trigger. Just a busted head and some stitches, to remind him not to ignore anything, even a bored perp playing with a bedrail. All in all, it was a pretty exciting couple of nights. It's a young man's game out there on the Mean Streets of New York City. Sergeant Cousin told his partner, "Only 17 years to go, Gordo." The partners got to go home for some rest, and it was back to work the next day.

Incident Two:

Shootout under the EL roadway and an Angel on officer Cousin's shoulder.

"Well," one cop used to say, "the night isn't over until you see the George Washington Bridge in your rear-view mirror."

That's the way it was in the good old days at PSA 6. Sometimes the busiest part of a tour occurs when you are in route to a post or going back to the precinct at the end of the shift. This time it was at about 2330 hrs. and Jay was just beginning the 12-block ride back to the station house to sign out for the night.

His assignment that tour was from the Polo Grounds Housing Project at 155th Street and Frederick Douglass Boulevard to the Drew Hamilton Housing Project at 143rd street and Frederick Douglass Boulevard (also known as 8th Avenue). Back in the late 1980s, the scenery on the trip from the projects back to the station house consisted of the same thing: bodegas and burned-out buildings. And, of course, the occasional Chinese takeout restaurant. On the corner of 155th Street and Frederick Douglass Boulevard, there was one of those mom-and-pop fried chicken joints. It always did a decent amount of business from the residents of the Polo Grounds Houses. There was also a steady drug trade going on in the parking lot there at night. Cousin was used to finding a lot of guns, drugs, addicts, and narcotic dealers, with the remains of chicken wing bones thrown on the sidewalk for good measure. He rarely came across a street crime scene without seeing some gnawed off chicken wing bones on the ground. That takeout restaurant made some good chicken wings. Officer Cousin and Gordo could attest to that.

Anyway, Jay started his return to the precinct from the 4 x12 tour. He was the Project's community officer at the Polo Grounds. He'd walk a solo foot post or drive his little three-wheel scooter around the area. Tonight, he was on the scoter. While driving back to command, the radio blurts out a job for shots fired at 155 and 8th Avenue, right by the chicken place. Jay was right in the vicinity. But he was by himself, but figured, why not? I'm right there and most of these shots fired calls are bullshit, anyway.

He turned onto 155th at 8th and all hell's breaking loose. There were shots going off everywhere. A perp on the Southeast corner of the lot, standing next to a parked vehicle, was firing at a guy driving a Jeep Cherokee which was traveling eastbound on 155th street, and passing under the EL Roadway. The perp in the Jeep was returning firing while he was driving toward the perp on the corner. The first subject kept popping up and down behind the parked car he's taking cover behind. As bad luck would have it, Jay found himself in the middle of the crossfire. He was exposed on the scooter and in desperate need of cover.

The perp on the corner (who was later identified as Smiley) pops off a good one and nails the driver of the jeep. He slumps over the steering wheel, severely injured.

Then the Cherokee runs headfirst into the underpass column with a sickening thud and crash. The horn was blaring.

Cousin managed to get out of his scooter and find shelter behind a steel girder pole under the L train. He turned and made eye contact with Smiley, who had his gun wheeling towards him. Officer Cousin trained his gun on Smiley, but he's sheltering behind the parked vehicle. He was about 30 feet away and hidden behind the car. All Cousin could see of the perp was from chest up.

It was dark, and the dark vehicle protected him from most angles. Officer Cousin knew it would take an excellent shot to nail him. Smiley dipped down one more time behind the parked car and Cousin wasn't sure if he was on the move. The horn from the Jeep was still blaring, making it impossible to hear footsteps. Cousin's heart was pounding like a racehorse. He was ready to blast that fuck and give him a well-needed dirt nap. All he needed was for him to come up one more time, and then he was prepared to fire a shot to stop the perp. Which we all know is a kill shot. Those idiotic sayings in the academy had no place in the street. You never shoot to stop an armed felon. You shoot to kill. That's the bottom line. You or him.

Officer Cousin kept his gun trained on on the perp at center mass. He was ready. Then the perp surprised him As he stood, Cousin could see his hands come up first; they were both empty. So, he held back from firing.

He had the perp place his hands on the hood and he immediately went towards him. Cousin was walking quickly but he always keeping his gun trained on him. A minute later, he grabbed Smiley and threw him against the parked vehicle. He was a skinny kid and didn't put up a fight. He had been shot once in his lower back but was still very mobile.

Officer Cousin cuffed him and waited for any unit available to come and get to him. It felt like it took forever. He could hear sirens and there was a huge crowd gathering in front of the chicken joint. Cousin later learned that someone had made a 911 call and said there was a cop getting shot at on 155th and 8th Avenue. He never discovered who was looking out for him.

Eventually, several units arrived, and he was relieved. A 32-Precinct Police officer walked up, and Cousin asked him to hold on to Smiley for a second.

He then went over to the parked car Smiley was taking cover behind and reached underneath and recovered Smiley's gun. He secured it and walked over to the Jeep. The driver was DOA, leaning against the steering wheel. He grabbed the gun from the floor of the vehicle and secured it, then returned to his captured perp. A cop from the 32nd pulled the plug on the damn horn of the Jeep, and things felt under control again. Smiley was taken to Harlem Hospital for treatment of his gunshot wound and kept under guard. The crime scene was established. Hours later, Officer Cousin returned to the precinct and started the beginning of a long period of arrest processing. He thought to himself. "I won't be seeing the George Washington Bridge in my rear-view mirror tonight."

But all in all, he felt pretty good that night.

Incident Three:

Rooftops, Rapes and Rescues.

Every cop who works in the projects knows the first rule. If the old timers talk to you when you come into the precinct, all green and spanking new, they might mumble, "Always look up, kid." That might be the only thing they tell you for another 5 years. That's entirely another story. They don't trust you and they got one eye, if not both eyes, on the exit and retirement. They basically look at you with that look and shake their heads and smile, then walk away, still shaking their heads and chuckling to themselves. Old timers in the New York housing police department went to work to fuck their mistresses in the projects, get a good meal cooked for them, and head back home for the night.

It was one of Jay's first midnight foot patrols in the Dyckman Houses, which are seven, fourteen-story low-income buildings, in Northern Manhattan. He was scoping out activity on the street from a rooftop on 10th Avenue. He looked down and saw a guy checking out parked vehicles. The subject was moving along, checking each vehicle. After a few minutes, he finally settled on one and began using a tool to open the door. He was the only guy on the street and officer Cousin raced down from the roof to catch him before he was in the wind. Cousin transmitted a GLA (Grand Larceny Auto) was in progress on his radio. But he didn't know if the dispatch or anyone else had heard him. There was no acknowledgement from anyone.

Officer cousin went down to the street and observed him sitting in the vehicle. He didn't seem to pay much attention to what was going on around him. Jay crouched down and moved closer, staying low enough not to be seen. He kept his back against each car, moving car by car until he came up behind the perp. The door was open, so he stuck his .38 revolver in his ear. The perpetrator was scared shitless. He had been fiddling around with a bunch of wires inside the steering column, attempting to hot-wire the vehicle. He was too scared to put up a fight. Officer Cousin quickly cuffed him and called for transport back to the station house. A 34 Precinct Sergeant and his driver responded and transported him back to his command.

Jay walked into the house with his collar and there was an old-time sergeant on the desk, and he was annoyed that Jay interrupted him at that ungodly hour. "What's this bullshit you have here?" the boss asked him.

Jay told him. "It's a guy breaking into cars from the Dyckman Houses."

"Oh, okay." The old timer changed his tune. He'd thought Jay had a nonsense trespass charge. He glared at the perp and said, "Got you. You son of a bitch!"

Car break-ins are a big item if you live in the city, as most of these old timers do. Officer Cousin had lived in the Bronx for a while, over near the Zoo. He was constantly going to Hunt's Point and buying back his stolen vent window. The thief knew he'd keep getting it back, so he kept stealing it from his old Ford Escort. There was nothing Cousin hated more than a car thief. To him, they were the bottom of the barrel.

Well, the old timer said to him, "Good collar, Cousin. An old timer would have been sleeping."

Jay earned a little respect from the old timers at that point. But not much. They were a hard bunch. But they had been correct on one thing. Watch out for those rooftops. You never know who or what is up there. And when it's nighttime, as soon as you open the door to the roof, you light up like a shooting range target and are at an extreme disadvantage. A lot of bad things happen on rooftops, from rapes to shootings to drug deals to simple pissing. But you have to be ready for anything. Your heart always jumps up in your throat when you find someone up there.

Incident Four:

One day, about 5 o'clock in the afternoon, officer Cousin was performing his first building vertical of his tour in the St Nicholas Projects. This wasn't a wonderful, family friendly neighborhood. The force referred to it as Vietnam. Cousin was doing a check of the roof landing when found an old uncle raping his two pre-teenage nieces.

Great collar, you would think. No one likes a pedophile. Until you arrest him and start walking him toward the transport vehicle. Then you have to watch out for airmail, especially when you're walking along a building. There's always shit coming out the windows directed at your ass. Empty bottles, bottles filled with piss, a bag full of diapers. Anything handy and as messy as possible.

Often, he was pelted by pieces of furniture. Once, while working the good old Polo Grounds late one night, a Molotov cocktail was thrown at him. Sure, it was a beautiful sight as it was hurled from one of the upper floors directly into the area where officer Cousin was walking his beat. The firebomb smashed against a wall. It was nice and bright, glowing like a comet as it fell to earth and shattered into flames at the base of the home plate. Right where there's a plaque affixed to the building to signify its historical significance of the old baseball team, the New York Giants. Cousin called it ball one. The fireball finally fizzled out. Talk about having an angel on your shoulder. That night, he could've been badly burned or even killed. Talk about having brass balls. Officer Cousin just kept pounding the Polo Grounds every day and night. It was his turf, not theirs.

Incident Five:

It was the late eighties and the introduction of crack-cocaine into the inner city had unleashed an unprecedented wave of drug addiction and violence. The bad guys were out of control in the Big Apple. Who had time for that type of crazy shit? The buildings in the projects were 30 floors high. A large percent of the residents were either out on parole or trying to make a name for themselves by creating mayhem in the Polo Grounds.

Most of the time, Officer Cousin just let it go. He was used to bottles and other things coming off the roof. Some of it could kill you. (*As it killed one of our cops in our command. That happened in Washington Heights. Poor John Williams, Rest in Peace Brother. He was an only child. His mother was rightfully devastated.*) Well, nothing prepared the officers for what came off a roof, right in front of Cousin and his partner.

One night on the late tour, about 3am or thereabouts, officer Cousin got a radio run of calls for help on 127th Street and Eighth Avenue, in the St. Nicholas Houses.

The two officers pulled up in front of the building and looked around. All was quiet. As they approached the doorway of the building, they heard a loud noise coming from above. Horrifying screams were growing louder. Then there was an incredible crash. It took them a second to comprehend what it was. Then the two cops realized a human body had just landed on the overhang of the entrance door. An arm dangled down off the side of the short overhang. The pale white arm was attached to a naked body.

As the startled officers looked at the body dangling

off the overhand, there was a loud thud as a firearm landed right beside him.

Officer Cousin immediately notified central. Within minutes, another unit had circled around to the exit doors of the back of the building. They apprehend one male fleeing out the door. This collar made the investigation much easier. No perp wants to take the heat of a murder alone. Within a few days, the other perps were apprehended. It was an interesting story.

Apparently, the white dude had been selling guns to the kids in the projects and the deal had gone literally south, really quick. The kids had forcefully removed the seller from his vehicle and brought him into the lobby of the building. They made him strip completely and then they threw his clothes in the trash compactor. They might have been satisfied by locking him on the rooftop without his clothing, but in the end a violent fight broke out as the seller realized his plight. He was outnumbered and easily overcome. Now the kids were mad, so off the roof he went. He fell fifteen floors and met his demise when his body struck the roof of the

building entrance. It is what it is, but that was a new one. You never see it all in this job. The rooftops had their fair share of jumpers as well. The thing about jumpers that complicated the job, is they always would take you with them if you tried to interfere with their plans.

Incident Six:

Cousin and his partner T-Rex had a pretty good routine going for them, but one night was a classic. It was during a violent thunderstorm. The partners got a radio run for someone on the roof at the Wagner Houses. The

Robert F. Wagner houses are 22 buildings in the East Harlem portion of Manhattan. Over 5000 people lived in the high-rise apartments, most of which were 15 stories tall.

It was late; sometime after midnight. The officers proceeded straight to the roof and out the door. Thunder and lightning lit up the sky. There was a female standing on the roof parapet in the pouring rain. She was screaming, as she held her arms and face raised towards heaven. The way she was jerking around and talking nonsense, it was clear she was getting ready to take the final dive. With the angry sky as a backdrop, she looked like the demon exiting Linda Blair's body. Cousin tried to talk her down as she got ready to take that last step. Nothing seemed to get through to her.

Finally, T–Rex signaled Cousin to distract her, so he screamed at her over the thunder and rain to come back off the ledge. T-Rex goes around to her rear and inches along the wall towards her. He was illuminated now and then by lightning, looking almost like a spider as he maintained his crouching position until he reached her. He signaled to Jay again and then quickly grabs her leg. Officer Cousin moved in to secure her arms and the fight was on. They struggled with this poor woman, but she wouldn't give up her plans easily. She was a fighter and tried desperately, using any means available, to take that dive. Th roof was wet and slick and all of them were soaked. It was extremely hard to keep a grip on the whacked-out woman, but they were able to haul her in and restrain her until the ambulance arrived. Job well done.

Or so, they thought.

A boss told them, "You should have waited for ESU."

Not, "Hey guys! Great work out here tonight. I'm

going to put you in for a medal." What the hell is that guy talking about? How could they have waited for ESU to come? There was no doubt she would have jumped to her death if they'd waited any longer. Officer Cousin was thinking to himself. "Kiss my ass. She was going to go over if we didn't grab her."

No doubt her family would agree.

Incident Seven:

This was the similar story in Corsi House on 117th street. A dispute between a mother and son. The partners arrive at the building and knock on the door of the apartment listed in the contact. The door opend and an older woman was standing there. Her eyes are extremely distraught as she looked at us and the sergeant, who was also on the scene.

This isn't a dispute; it was an imminent suicide. The woman's middle-aged son was straddling the bedroom window, one leg in and one leg out. It was easy to see he was ready to go. The mother was begging him to come back inside the apartment.

He wasn't paying her any attention.

Officer Cousin always had a soft spot for jumpers. He took in the scene and realized there was no time to waste. The man was about 20 feet from him. As he turned his head to look one more time down to the street and work his courage up, Cousin saw his opportunity. He sprinted the twenty feet to the guy, and he wasn't playing around. He grabbed the distraught man by the waist in a football crouch and literally hauled him right out of his shoes and onto the floor. He was quickly cuffed for his own safety and transported for medical evaluation. The man was pissed, but at least his life was saved for that day. Again, the boss told Officer Cousin, "You should've waited for ESU." Later that night the Sergeant called officer Cousin's wife at home to tell her what a great job he thought Cousin did. Sergeant Cousin never forgot that small gesture.

Incident Eight:

The hardest cases Sergeant Cousin had to work were the sexual assaults and rapes. Unfortunately, these types of calls occurred much too often to avoid. Many times, Cousin had to handle working a solo foot post at the Polo Ground Houses. The Polo Ground Complex was four thirty-story towers, with almost 2000 residents, a lot of territory for one man to patrol on his own.

One day shift, officer Cousin got a call for a rape in progress, along with a description of the male. He responded to the call and spotted the perp coming right out the front door of the 2979 side of the building. He was strutting, feeling pretty good about something. The first thing Cousin saw was the jailhouse tats. That usually meant he had done serious time. He was built like a linebacker, heavily muscled like many men who have nothing much to do with their time inside. He sees officer Cousin walking that way and makes a u turn, running back into the building.

Officer Cousin had played this game before. He quickly runs around to the 2971 side and waited. Seconds later, the perp came running out. Cousin dives into him and it's on. This guy was a bull. Officer Cousin knew it was quite possible the man would overpower him quickly. He could never figure out the reason, but after a brief struggle, the perp stopped resisting, and Cousin cuffed him. Other units arrived and officer Cousin headed up to the crime scene. The perp had knocked on the door of an acquaintance that wasn't home. When he discovered the 16-year-old relative was at home alone, he forced his way into the apartment. Once inside, he tied her to the bed and raped her. She was a beautiful young girl, and the sexual predator was in his mid-thirties. The ropes were still attached to the bedposts. The sadistic pervert went down for 30 years on that rape. Maybe he just wanted to go back to jail, or maybe he knew hell was coming after him if he didn't.

Incident Nine:

Officer Cousin and his partner T-Rex were working a late tour when another unit handled a rape early in the shift and broadcasted a description of the assailant. They were just killing time near a local watering hold since they regularly caught a call there around closing time. You can imagine their surprise when, just after 3am, the wanted felon comes walking out of the bar at 145th Street and 8th Avenue. Sergeant Cousin said he'll never forget this collar, because Leslie West had just started playing *Theme for an Imaginary Western* on the radio and that song is one of his favorites. Officer Cousin made eye contact with the perp and the chase was on. He jumped out of the RMP and hauled ass after him. T-Rex followed in the car. The guy ran down 146th street and poof he was gone.

Officer Cousin knew the perp hadn't had enough time to get far. He had to be hiding nearby. He began a search. His partner moved about half the block up the street and began working his way back toward Cousin. It didn't take long before Officer Cousin spotted his legs sticking out from underneath a car. He signaled for his partner, and the two men dragged him out from underneath a parked car. He was another stocky guy, but there were two of them and not enough of him. So now Cousin and T-Rex had another perp under for rape.

A great collar, and all was right with the world for the time being.

That may've been one of the last good collars Cousin and T-Rex had, as the writing was on the wall. A short time later, they went their separate ways. Officer Cousin moved into the Bronx shortly before getting promoted. Cousin and T had a lot of great collars, and they were looking to make some money on the late tour with all the overtime from the arrests they were making. T loved his midnights. They were getting to be the old timers by then. The job will do that to you.

I know Sergeant Cousin personally and he's one of the few I'd want by my side in the heat of battle. He always had every police officer's six, and to this day has mine. Sergeant Cousin, thank you, for your service and dedication to the city of New York. Godspeed brother...

The following dedication was written by Sergeant Jay Cousin, and Pete Thron contributed.

"The Ones we've lost and The Street Angels"

You learn quickly that the streets show no favoritism just because you wear a uniform. The streets are a cold place, and you don't see a lot of the so-called beauty of the job. You're dealing primarily with the lost, the forgotten, and the criminals. These are just the dark, iniquity elements a police officer must face every tour they work. After a while, you begin to think that this is all that exists when doing the job. A police officer tries hard to re-adjust their thinking, but sometimes that perception can get you killed or thrown in jail.

Criminals are master manipulators, and most have been that way a great portion of their lives. It is the way of the street. As I heard one cop say, he doesn't like to act from a place of defense. I believe this to be true. But in this day and age, law enforcement officers must act on the defensive side, rather than the offensive side of the ball. The game has been rigged by the politicians and the justice system, who are just covering their asses. I've spoken to several cops, district attorneys, and judges that aren't in agreement with these rules. Their hands are tied.

Early in his career, Jay was assigned to guard a prisoner at Harlem Hospital on the late shift one night. A career criminal who was in his 40s was the perpetrator Jay was guarding. Every part of the defendant's body showed life in the streets. He'd been shot and stabbed on several occasions. His body had all the scars to prove it. Jay thought to himself. "This guy knows more ways to kill me than I ever knew existed. He was old for a street warrior and a survivor. He was an odds beater and past his life expectancy." Like policing, living a life of crime is a young man's game and sooner or later it'll catch up to you. A lot of police officers were shot and killed during Jay's 20-year career in the NYPD. But several of them seem to stick in his mind. I know several of the officer's Jay has written about, and their deaths have always left a deep wound in my heart and memory. As it has Jay's. These hit home more than others for Jay's personal reasons. Those are the demons Jay must deal with every day.

Shortly after Jay entered the Academy in 1984, a young cop was in a gas station on 149th street and Bruckner Boulevard, a busy high crime area in the Bronx. The officer was shot in the head and killed while attempting to question a male on a stolen motorbike. Officer Thomas Ruotolo only had 3 years on the job. His partner was also shot but survived. An off-duty cop on a pay phone at the gas station exchanged gunfire with the perp and he was also shot. The perpetrator was a violent career criminal. During the gun battle, while exchanging shots with the police, he'd also been wounded. He fled the scene, but he desperately needed medical attention and went to a hospital. The defendant was arrested and taken into custody after receiving medical treatment. He'll be eligible for parole in 2 years. Turns out the murdered police officer was a friend of Jay's brother-in-law. His wife survived him. That one stuck in Jay's mind because it just showed how quick it can happen and how senseless it can be. The streets don't care who you are. They will kill you.

A few months after graduating from the academy, Jay was assigned to a foot post on 10th Avenue in Upper Manhattan. It was a beautiful clear autumn day; the skies were bright blue, and the air was crisp. He could smell the aroma of the leaves on the ground. As officer Cousin walked his day shift, patrolling the project grounds, he could hear the number 1 NE train rumble over his head. There was terrible news being transmitted over the radio from central. "Transit officer Irma Lozada has become the first female NYC police officer ever to be killed in the line of duty." She was murdered with her own gun. Officer Lozada was assigned to Transit District 33 working a plain clothes detail in Brooklyn. She was part of the Transit Decoy Unit and was attempting to apprehend a perpetrator who'd committed a chain snatch robbery. Officer Lozada was a beautiful young officer with 4 years on the job at the time of her murder. She was survived by her mother and brother, who was an NYPD auxiliary cop.

The violent inmate who'd assassinated officer Lozada in 1984 was quietly released from prison during the month of December 2021, by Andrew Cuomo's parole board.

As I stated, there were many officers killed over Jay's 20- year career. All of them were heroes and should be honored every day. This dedication could go on for days. It's a book in itself.

For unknown personal reasons, these are the ones that stuck in Jay's mind. Officer Scott Gadell in June 1986 was killed in Far Rockaway as he reloaded his revolver while engaged in a shootout with a suspect who was out on bail from a 1985 drug related murder. That defendant had been threatening another man with a pistol. Scott had been a U.S. Army reserve veteran and had been a police officer for only a year. He's parents survived him. His killer was paroled in June 2021 by the disgraced, ex-mayor Andrew Cuomo's parole board under the New York Bail Reform Law.

At the time of officer Gadell's murder, NYPD officers were severely outgunned and still carrying six shot revolvers. While many perpetrators on the street were carrying high-capacity automatic weapons. His murder was an impetus for NYPD to improve their standards for officers and to prevent their adversaries from having a clear advantage in weapons over the officers.

In June 1988, Officer Gary Peaco was killed on the Grand Concourse in the Bronx as he responded to a

10- 13 from two NYPD officers engaged in a shootout with 4 robbery suspects. Officer Peaco's RMP was struck by an ambulance, which caused it to spin out of control, strike a lamppost, and burst into flames. Officer Peaco was ejected from the vehicle and landed 30 feet away. His injuries were fatal. He was survived by his wife and twin daughters.

Jay wore his memorial bar on his shield holder until the day he retired.

The list goes on and on. Eddie Byrne. Michael Buczek and Christopher Hoban were both killed within minutes of each other in Uptown, Manhattan. They worked in different commands that covered Harlem and Washington Heights. I'd also been working that night with my partner, and I'll tell you firsthand, it was total fucking chaos. Their funeral was held at the same time. Police officers from throughout the country showed up to pay their respects. Over 12,000 law enforcement officers came to mourn their deaths, filling the church on 60th street and Fifth Avenue. That's a day I'll never forget. It's burned into my memory and soul forever.

Officer John Williamson, whom Jay had served as his FTO (field training officer). John was murdered senselessly in Upper Manhattan and for no apparent reason, if there ever is a reason.

Officer Hector Fontanez, Officer Sean McDonald, and officer Vincent Guidice, all gave their lives in service to the community they swore to protect.

Then came the horrible September 11th, 2001, terrorist attack and its aftermath, the effects of which we still see today.

Close to 100 NYPD officers were killed in the line of duty during Jay's career. The toll was staggering, and the funerals were endless. The heartbreak that resulted from these deaths is immeasurable. Jay possessed something at the beginning of his career, which he no longer possessed after 20 years. There was a part of him which no longer existed. If you've experienced and seen the horrors that so many cops see day in and day out, you'll understand why we've become numb to death. These feelings can't be named. They are just a part of an officer's soul. We'll leave it unnamed at this point, however its absence is apparent. But Jay Cousin, along with countless other NYPD officers, as well as police officers throughout the world, will tell you, being a cop is the best thing they ever did. Jay wouldn't change a minute of it.

But the streets were not without hope and angels without wings did and do, exist. A few years later, while walking a foot post around the Polo Ground Towers, an armed cab robbery on 155th Street and Bradhurst Avenue came over the radio. Officer Cousin saw a male fleeing the scene, and he started to pursue him on foot. He didn't have time to put the pursuit over the radio. The subject fled directly through the project grounds and onto Eighth Avenue. The cop and robber passed by numerous residents and most of them went on as if it was just another day in the hood. The perp tossed an object into a trash can as he continued running down the Avenue. He made a left turn down a walkway between a community center and a building. He was headed for Building 4, aka Vietnam, in the Polo Grounds. Jay overtook him. Both men were winded and exhausted from the foot pursuit.

Officer Cousin threw the perp against a black steel barred fence. Now the battle was on. They were grappling and fighting fist to cuffs. Jay was having a tough time restraining him and couldn't cuff him. Finally, the cavalry showed up and placed the felon in custody. Officer Cousin was spent and bleary from the chase and physical altercation, but knew his day was just starting. The object thrown in the trashcan had disappeared. Weapons that are tossed by perps always have legs and find their way to another criminal. He expected that weapon would also vanish into the Belly of The Beast.

There was a street angel in the area that day. Someone, and Jay never found out who it was, had made an anonymous call, saying that there was a cop chasing a suspect on Eighth Avenue in front of the Polo Grounds and was engaged in a fight. That call might have saved his life. There are street angels out there.

One warm summer night on 143rd street and Eighth Avenue as Jay was heading out to patrol, a gorgeous dark-skinned female with a beautiful smile approached him in the street. She asked him. "Do you remember me?"

For the life of him, he couldn't. She went on to thank Jay for saving her life. She then reminded the officer who she was, and it all came back to him. She'd been a serious crack addict in the projects on 155th street and she credited officer Cousin with saving her life. They had a few previous encounters where he'd found her in numerous crack dens. But she'd turned her life around and thanked him for helping her do just that. It was moments like that which made everything worthwhile. Simple things at the most unexpected times.

One day, Jay was in a RadioShack back in the early 90s in Upstate NY. There was a long line as the manager of the store worked the register. Officer Cousin was watching a male scoping out some VCRs. He observed the man pick one up and start to walk out the door. The manager was occupied and didn't notice. Jay told the manager what had just transpired. Then his instincts kicked in, and he ran out after the perp. Why he did that is still a mystery. I can tell you why. It's in a cop's blood to help and protect people 24-7.

Jay caught up to the guy and asked him if he'd paid for the VCR. The bastard threw the VCR at Jay's head and a second later they're in an all-out brawl on the street. Jay was wondering, "how am I going to secure this guy? I have no cuffs and we're both rolling around on the asphalt and getting all cut up. " Out of nowhere, a guy appeared, and Jay asked him, "Can you give me a hand?" He turned out to be an off-duty State Trooper. Another street angel.

Officer Cousin actually got a commendation letter from the chief of the Middletown Police department for that arrest.

Jay has been retired 18 years now, and it seems like another lifetime ago. One day goes into the next, and some of the names and memories are beginning to fade. They always say the 20 years go quickly, but they fail to say retirement goes just as fast. The world has changed so much he scarcely recognizes it. Some of the old friends have passed with many succumbing to 911 related illnesses. Jay often thinks back to when we were so green, young, and new in the academy so many years ago. There are two things of which he and I are certain and will never be convinced of otherwise. One is there's a God in heaven. The other is that Jay was an admirable NYPD cop, and he made a difference. These two beliefs will never be taken from us. God Bless and stay safe.

Chapter Fourteen

Retired NYPD Detective Second Grade:

Ralph Friedman

Ralph is the Co-Author of the bestselling book 'Street Warrior', and several of his incredible arrests have been featured and aired on two major networks: The Discovery Channel and the I.D. Channel. The series 'Street Justice the Bronx' is now featured on multiple networks including Amazon prime. Each episode runs an hour long in length. There are six episodes featuring parts of Ralph's career. As of this writing, the show hasn't been canceled and still has a possibility of being renewed. If it wasn't renewed, it was most likely due to the anti-police sentiment that set in after the first season.

Ralph's arrest statistics as a cop and detective are staggering. He made over 2000 solo arrests and assisted in another 6000 collars. He also made 105 off-duty arrests, ranging from narcotic sales to homicides in progress. Ralph was involved in 15 shootings, which resulted in 8 criminals being shot, including four being killed during the gun battles. Ralph has killed more violent criminals in the line of duty than any officer living today. He's the most decorated detective in the history of the NYPD. He served during one of the city's most dire period: the 1970s and 80s. During that time, heavily armed gangs controlled the corners of the Bronx, Brooklyn, Queens, and Manhattan. If you've ever watched the movie 'The Warriors,' then you probably have a good idea of the time. Ralph was a cop in areas many consider Hell on earth. He worked in the notorious 41st precinct, also known as Fort Apache. That command was so dangerous and had such a reputation for extreme violence that Hollywood made a motion picture of it. When he was Grade, he remained in the Bronx area.

Detective Friedman was also partnered with the highly decorated detective, Timothy Kennedy, who Ralph said was his best detective partner ever. (Tim Kennedy is featured in chapter 9 and is also chapter 9 in Ralph's book). I'm good friends with both heroes and I can tell you firsthand, there are no other cops you'd feel safer with in the field of battle. Together they rained terror onto the drug pushers and gun toting scumbags that tried to terrorize the citizens of the Bronx.

Ralph had a knack of knowing when a perp was

about to commit a crime before it happened. He worked in the anti-crime unit in plainclothes for most of his career, even as a detective. He needed to be in the street, not sitting behind a desk waiting for an incident to occur. Ralph wanted to be in the trenches with the other cops and detectives that pounded the beat. Detective Friedman made more collars than most plain clothes units combined. His career was cut short when he was responding to a 10-13 (officer needs assistance). His unmarked car was struck by another uniform patrol car, also responding to the 10-13. Ironically, detective Kennedy was driving the car detective Friedman was in. All four officers involved in the accident were injured. Three of the officers were treated and released the next day. If Friedman hadn't been in the shape that he was in, he would've been killed in the accident. During the collision, he suffered 23 broken bones; including a shattered right hip, broken pelvic bone on the left, and right, upper and lower ribs. After the accident, he was placed in traction for two and a half months, and then spent weeks in a wheelchair. After several months, Friedman was finally walking on crutches. Luckily, he was and is still a weight training fanatic. The doctors that treated him said, "Detective Friedman, if you weren't in the physical condition you are in today, you never would have survived the crash."

Detective Friedman was forced to retire because of his injuries. His career lasted 14 years (not including the 2 years serving as a police trainee due to age requirements). The accomplishments that he has are truly amazing. I often wonder how many more collars and medals he would've made and received had he worked a full 20-year career or more.

Incident One:
Why No Medal Day Ceremony?

November 1st, 1972, officer Friedman was assigned to the anti-crime unit of the 41st precinct. Few cops can say that they'd been handpicked to be in that unit within a two-year span of being on patrol. But Friedman had earned the respect of his commanding officer with all the collars he'd brought in. That morning, he headed down to the Bronx Criminal Court building to testify at a grand jury on a collar he'd made earlier that week. Another member of the anti-crime team, officer Unger, also had a court date. After they'd finished with their respective cases, they headed back to the command. Experience shows that most police officers would either bang out for the rest of their tour or try to drag out their case at court until the end of their shifts. But the cops who were considered the Five Percenters preferred to back into their uniforms or unmarked cars and hit the streets to make more collars. That's exactly what officer Friedman and Unger did. They jumped into one of their personal vehicles and hit the Bronx streets, on the hunt for anyone about to commit a crime or was committing one. They didn't expect to wait long; officer Friedman was what most cops call *a magnet for guns*.

At 1355 hours they were cruising down Westchester Avenue near Fox Street, when they heard a signal 10-31 (Burglary in Progress) being transmitted over the air by the communications dispatcher. It was a radio run for patrol, but officer Friedman and officer Unger backed them up. The crime units would often do that in heavier crime areas. The call was at 992 Fox Street on the roof of the building. Friedman and his partner were just a few buildings away, and they swung into action. The blood pumped in his veins as they pulled up to the location. Ralph told central. "Central 41-crime is on the scene and will back up 41-Adam. Is there an apartment, or a complainant connected to the 10-31?"

Central advised Ralph that the call had just escalated into a woman screaming for help. "Put us on the scene handling the job central."

A call like that means that imminent danger is happening to a person, and it's escalated into an extremely dangerous situation and has become urgent. "Central notify any responding officers that there are two plainclothes officers on the scene."

"10-4, 41 Crime."

They proceeded up the stairs quickly, but with great caution. When an officer that works in plain clothes responds to a crime in progress, he must be diligent and have eyes in the back of his head. Plain clothes cops aren't wearing uniforms, so they can easily be mistaken as the bad guy by another uniform cop. It's an incredibly dangerous unit to work in.

Upon reaching the 5th floor, which was also the last floor before the roof landing, Officers Friedman and Unger observed the door to apartment 5E was badly damaged and standing open approximately 7 inches. Both officers had already taken their weapons out and approached the door with as much stealth as humanly possible. They could hear a woman screaming for help inside the apartment. Friedman knew she was in some serious trouble. She could be getting assaulted and battered. When they entered the apartment, they could see it was pitch black inside due to blankets, sheets, and shades covering the windows. Not a bit of sunlight came through the apartment. No house lights were on in the dwelling, either. The two officers were entering a kill box.

In officer Friedman's mind, the increased danger just added fuel to the fire. Her screams continued while they forged ahead in the darkness. The partners could hear the crunching of the cockroaches as they stepped on the filthy floor. The screams were coming from the rear of the apartment. As they navigated through the darkness of the kill box, a subject later identified as Charles Williams emerged. He leapt in front of the officers and began firing his weapon. Multiple shots rang out, the flashes illuminating the darkness inside the apartment in a strobe-like atmosphere. The shots had been fired at them at point blank range. Officer Unger was hit by the several bullets but returned fire as he fell to the floor. Williams ran past officer Unger and fired two more shots at Officer Friedman, who used the illumination of rounds being fired at him to his advantage and returned fire. Officer Friedman returned fire from his revolver in the perp's direction, making sure they would hit him in the center mass area of his body. The perpetrator crashed into Ralph with his weapon still in hand, and officer Friedman responded, firing one last shot that dropped the violent felon, killing him.

Officer Friedman raced over to his partner, who lay dying on the floor. He immediately applied pressure to the gunshot wounds that riddled officer Unger's body. At the same time, he called for help over his walkie talkie. Seconds later, the cavalry arrived and took officer Unger down the stairs, opting not to wait for an ambulance to arrive. They rushed him in a marked patrol car to Jacobi Hospital, while other officers took care of the injured woman. Officer Unger was in critical condition and received 72 pints of blood in a three-hour span from members of the service and hospital personnel. The amount of blood that was lost and given to him made medical history. Officer Unger survived those wounds and is living today thanks to the quick instinctive reactions of officer Friedman and the responding uniform members of the service. A high-ranking boss and a Bronx trustee of the PBA told Friedman in the presence of several cops, "You're going to be promoted to detective and get the Medal of Honor for this."

That night, Friedman was going to hold a press conference at Jacobi Hospital. Prior to him speaking, Mayor Lindsey was flown in by helicopter from Manhattan. He landed on the street, on Pelham Parkway in front of the hospital, to check on officer Unger and to congratulate officer Friedman on his act of bravery.

Neither officer received the Medal of Honor or The Combat Cross, they rightfully deserved. Nor did they receive an invitation to Medal Day! They received an Honorable Mention Medal to put on their shield holders.

The shootout that these two officers were involved in occurred while they were within 3 feet of each other and often closer. It was in an enclosed pitch-black hallway. Not only were the bullets being fired at them; they were also ricocheting off the walls. The only light that was available for them to navigate was the gunpowder flash coming out of the weapons being fired. This was a time where their training kicked in and instincts took over until they stopped the deadly threat. The fearlessness they showed was beyond the call of duty. Thank God, they made it out alive. Officer Friedman was credited with the kill in action and for saving another officer's life, the victim of the burglary, and his own life. That incident is 100 percent worthy of the Medal of Honor, or at a minimum, the Combat Cross. For some unknown reason, they were not given any of those medals for that violent shootout. "Why no medals remain a mystery to this day?"

Incident Two:

November 9, 1974, officer Friedman was working in plainclothes on the late-night tour with his partner, officer Bobby Dematas. At approximately 0030 hours, while they were on patrol in an undercover yellow taxicab, cruising in the vicinity of East 149th Street and Southern Boulevard. As they passed the building, the partners observed four youths whose behavior caught both of the experienced officer's suspicions. They decided to put the young men under observation.

Ralph's radar was alerted by the way they were conducting themselves. The group started walking down the street. After a few minutes, they stopped in front of a building, 568 Prospect Avenue, and engaged in a conversation with a man who was later identified as Johnny Castro. As they were talking with the man, something changed in their conversation. Castro pulled out a .38-caliber revolver and fired two rounds at close range into one youth's chest, causing the other three youths to flee.

Officer Friedman gunned the taxi across four lanes of traffic, rolling right up to the scene. He and his partner jumped out of their vehicle and shouted, "Police, freeze."

Castro responded by firing at the officers while he fled up Fox Street. Officer Friedman fired at Castro while pursuing on foot. Officer Dematas called a 10-13 for the victim that was shot and then outflanked Castro to triangulate him in. The perp crouched down behind a parked vehicle to reload his .38. Then he alternated his shots at the officers. Officer Friedman unloaded his service revolver at Castro. Then he went to his backup revolver and fired four rounds from his off duty. Officer Dematas fired one round at the perp, hitting him in the shoulder. This resulted in Castro going down to the ground. Ralph rushed towards the fallen man to seize the opportunity to disarm him. However, when officer Friedman reached him, Castro raised his weapon and took aim at him. Friedman then fired one more shot into his head, killing him instantly. It was later ascertained that officer Friedman had hit Castro six times, but Dematas shot to the shoulder was the straw that broke the camel's back. Ralph had made a tight grouping in the perp's torso with the rounds he'd fired, but Castro's adrenaline, along with all the drugs and alcohol, had kept him going. Officer Friedman was credited with his second kill in action. Fox Street wasn't notoriously known for its violence, yet ironically, it was where Officer Friedman had his first two kills.

During the investigation, it was revealed that firearm Castro used had been stolen from Connecticut. Recovered at the scene next to his body were six spent shells and three live rounds, and three more that had been fired. The bullets were .38-caliber super-velocity hollow points. In total, there were more than 20 shots exchanged between the perp and the two officers. The 15-year-old victim that Castro had shot was rushed to Lincoln Hospital. The doctors performed surgery and removed two bullets from the young man. He was listed in critical condition from those gunshot wounds but survived due to the fast-acting officers calling for an ambulance. Ralph's commanding officer wrote this in his request for departmental recognition for officer Friedman and officer Dematas. "It's my opinion that the above-mentioned officers performed an act of extraordinary bravery, intelligently in the line of duty, at imminent and personal danger to life. Their unhesitant display of devotion to duty and the department brings the highest credit to themselves and to the 41st precinct. It's without hesitation that I recommend them for departmental recognition."

For their heroic actions, officers Friedman and Dematas received the Department Combat Cross on Medal Day.

Incident Three:

On December 23rd, 1978, Detective Friedman was assigned to the 52nd precinct Investigation Unit. It was his regular day off and he was spending it with his girlfriend and her sister. The two girls third sister lived 2025 Continental Avenue in the Bronx. As detective Friedman entered the building, he observed two males exiting the lobby and noticed one male had a gun in his waistband. Friedman quickly drew his weapon from his ankle holster and took his shield from his pocket and asked the man to produce a shield or permit for the weapon.

The man responded with, "What gun?"

During that time of questioning, the man moved his coat and closed it to conceal the gun. At that point, detective Friedman reached into the man's coat and removed the weapon, which was loaded and told the subject he was under arrest. The second individual continued to walk away. As detective Friedman informed the perpetrator that he was being arrested for possession of a firearm, the man told detective Friedman. "Look man, I have a couple of thousand dollars on me. Take a thousand from my pocket and keep it for yourself. Just let me go free. I'll throw the gun away."

While this was occurring, one of the sisters called

911 and told them what was transpiring. Minutes later, a radio patrol car arrived on the scene and escorted the perp back to the 45th precinct. It should be noted that the responding officer was none other than officer Tim Kennedy, who had heard of Ralph Friedman but never met him. Little did either of them know that three years down the road they'd become partners, making hundreds of felony collars together.

As officer Friedman was getting ready to leave the scene in his personal car, his girlfriend's sister said. "The second guy that kept walking, pulled out a gun and put it under a bush right next to our sister's building." Friedman checked the area where she'd told him the man had hidden the gun. Sure enough, he recovered another loaded firearm hidden in the bushes. For some reason, the second guy was still lingering in the area. Detective Friedman apprehended him and placed him under arrest. Another radio patrol car came to the scene and transported that perp to the 45th precinct.

I'll say one thing. Ralph wasn't a dull date. Ralph had made several arrests while on dates with other girls.

In the 45th station house under the supervision of the desk officer, I.A.D. was notified of the arrest, which included the bribery charge. The first weapon recovered was a Smith and Wesson .38-caliber revolver, which was fully loaded with .38 caliber ammo. The second gun was also a .38-caliber revolver, but the model was a Colt Cobra. It was loaded with four rounds of .38 caliber ammo.

Both men were already known to the department for their past criminal history. The first man, Carmine Dellacava, was a member of the Purple Gang and had family ties to one of the five families. He was also a suspect, along with another man, for the murder of Lennard

Flippone. Carmine's father is Stephen Dellacava, who was a well-documented Federal narcotics violator. He was serving time in a federal prison for narcotics and previous weapon violations.

The second perp that Ralph collared was Richard Malisia who'd been arrested previously for an Auto grand larceny and burglars' tools charge. He'd served one and half years on the charges. He'd also been arrested for helping in the escape of his father, Ernest (Pontiac) Malisia from the Federal House of Detention in Manhattan. Ernest Malisia was described by the federal authorities as one of the biggest narcotic dealers ever captured and arrested in the Metropolitan area. The apple didn't fall far from the tree.

The second perp, Richard Malisia, was wanted by the 5th Homicide Zone for a murder that had occurred on December 19th, 1978. Four days prior to detective Friedman collaring him, he'd killed William (Goldfinger) Terrel and wounded his brother Harry Terrel. The Terrel brothers were both big-time- narcotic dealers in the New York area. The young black men were the reputed successors of the jailed chieftain Leroy (Nicky) Barnes. The murder and attempted murder were apparently part of the current struggle between the Italian mob and the Black mob for control of the narcotic drug market in Harlem, New York. Richard Malisia was arrested again several days later for the murder and attempted murder of the Terrel brothers by the 5th Homicide Zone.

A police officer never really knows how dangerous an individual is who they're approaching or arresting. The commanding officer of the 45th wrote Ralph up for a medal and couldn't praise him enough for his courageous bravery. Ask yourself how dedicated Ralph was to the job, even when he was off duty, to disarm and apprehend two mafia hitmen while on a date with his girlfriend and sister.

Without a doubt, Detective Friedman was a Street Warrior and true hunter of evil. The arrests he made during his era have made history within the department and throughout our country. Detective Friedman is a household name and is a living legend within the law enforcement community. Throughout his 14-year career, he amassed 219 department awards and almost 40 civilian awards. He was awarded the Distinguished Service Award from Washington D.C. That medal is only given out to one officer every year. I want to say. Thank you for your dedication and service on and off-duty. You're the kind of police officer that New York City not only needs but demands in today's climate.

Thank you for reading Second to None, Book III the End of Tour Series.

If you enjoyed this book, I would greatly appreciate it, if you would leave a review on the retailer where you bougt it, and/or on a review site like Goodreads.

Once again, Thank you for reading my books!"

Join me on Facebook

https://www.facebook.com/petet3120

About the Author

Pete Thron was born and raised in Long Island, New York. He was a New York City Housing police officer for nearly a decade during the era of crack cocaine. During his time as a cop, he encountered some of the most violent and deadly drug organizations in New York City. He personally made over 600 arrests and assisted in over a thousand others. He was awarded over 100 medals and written commendations for bravery and successful convictions of violent offenders. He also worked as an investigator and fugitive recovery agent for nearly a decade. He has three children and is a grandparent. He currently works as a sports consultant and is the author of the End of Tour series.

Made in the USA
Middletown, DE
28 September 2022